FINDING CHRIST IN CRISIS

Lessons We Learned from COVID-19

Frank Santora

Frank Santora Ministries
600 Danbury Road, New Milford, CT 06776
www.franksantora.cc

ISBN: 9798666517543
Printed in the United States of America
©2020 by Frank Santora. All Rights Reserved.

CONTENTS

LESSON ONE
Never Waste a Good Crisis

The year 2020 just may go down in recent history as one of mankind's most difficult. The world-wide global pandemic caused an economic meltdown and collateral damage that we may never fully know or understand. Indeed, COVID-19 has been a storm to beat all storms. And as we continue to recover and move on with our lives, we cannot help but notice how we have been changed by the experience. Many focus on what we have lost: jobs, small businesses, economic stability, social relationships, loved-ones, mental, physical and emotional health... But let me remind you of what Philippians 4:8 says:

Finally, brethren, whatever things are true, whatever things are noble, whatever things are just, whatever things are pure, whatever things are lovely, whatever things are of good report, if there is any virtue and if there is anything praiseworthy—meditate on these things.

God's will for us is to focus on what is "good," regardless of circumstances. In this crisis, and in every crisis we will face in the future, there is good that can and will come out of it, especially when we remain faithful.

There's a business model that has been bantered about in the political arena lately, known simply as, "Never waste a good crisis." Essentially, the idea is that the best leaders use a crisis as an opportunity for massive change, without experiencing the usual resistance from people. During a sudden, unexpected crisis, an organization can make sweeping, wholesale changes as it adapts to the crisis—leading ultimately to rapid improvements overall. The "fire" of the crisis provides the opportunity to rebuild better, faster. Would it surprise you to know that this business model is Biblical? I believe that it is the essence of Romans 8:28, my favorite Scripture:

And we know that all things work together for good to those who love God, to those who are the called according to His purpose.

COVID-19 was not sent by God. As long as we are in the Dispensation (or Age) of Grace, we can rightly say that God does not pour out His judgments on humanity. This pandemic came straight from the pit of Hell, and its author is the enemy of our souls. This crisis was created to take us down and out. But God can and will bring good out of it according to Romans 8:28. Indeed, God won't waste a good crisis!

This book has been developed in the heat of the fire of COVID-19. As we all made our way through months of quarantine and the careful reopening of our economy, the Holy Spirit continually spoke to me about the "good" that can come of this crisis through the lessons that we have learned in the process. As you work though each of these lessons, I encourage you to reflect on your own experiences during this time, and ask yourself, how can you apply God's wisdom to your life in the future?

Probably the first lesson we all learned, is that we simply cannot take our lives for granted. Things can and do change suddenly, and can forever alter our experience of life. COVID-19 changed the face of our economy, our social relationships, and our educational process. We have adapted, but did we take advantage of these changes? What good has come out of the changes we have made personally?

I think it has also become apparent that not everyone has reacted to the crisis in the same manner. People will approach a crisis with certain preconceived opinions that will color what they believe and how they react. Sociologists call this a "worldview," and it determines to a large extent how people get through a crisis. For example, your worldview will filter the facts and determine whether you see doctors and politicians as heroes or tyrants. But as Bible-believing Christians, we have one worldview that is true, and we must avoid getting caught up in the worldview of those on the nightly news. Do you know what God says in His Word about how we should react to a crisis?

Certainly, a spirit of fear has gripped the world during this pandemic, and will likely do so until a vaccine is created. Don't misunderstand me... fear is a real human emotion. However, we know politicians use fear for political control, and the media uses fear to generate ratings. Most importantly, the devil uses fear to steal victory from God's people. God says fear is being "faithless", and we cannot please God, or have the victory, without having faith. But have you learned how to get past all the fear-mongering and look at your circumstance with the eyes of faith instead of fear?

Fear can take over when faith is weak. But it's difficult to know where your faith is when you are "smooth sailing" through life on calm seas. COVID-19 has been a storm of great proportions, and it suddenly revealed to everyone just how strong their faith was. Generally, the strength of one's faith in crisis is determined beforehand by the strength of your relationship with God. It is also greatly affected by your understanding of who you are to Him. When you are in Christ, and He is in you, no devil in hell can take you out! If you are completely confident of your identity in Christ, you will be able to face COVID-19 and every other crisis that comes your way. So if you need to build your faith, where should you begin?

For all of us, this crisis has caused permanent changes, and some are especially damaging. Social distancing has forced us to isolate from each other, keep six feet apart, and cover our faces. And suddenly, we are aware of what we have been taking for granted... the assembling of ourselves in worship on a Sunday morning. Before the COVID-19 crisis, we would think nothing of skipping church if we had a conflict with youth sports or some event. (Indeed, many only showed up 1.7x a month!)

But in quarantine, all such gathering was suddenly forbidden: joining together in worship, loving and hugging each other in friendship and in compassion, laying on hands and praying for the sick. We've suddenly discovered the fact that we were created to be in community with one another. As the Body of Christ, we function as a whole unit, each part doing what it was created to do, and we are simply better together. How do we ensure we never separate ourselves from each other, or from God, again?

It's easy to be discouraged by adverse circumstances. Going through a crisis of any sort is stressful and exhausting... physically, mentally and emotionally. But if we learned anything from our forced shut down, it's that our pre-COVID-19 daily life was too hectic! So many of us were forced to stay at home that we finally had time to take a long look at our crazy-fast lifestyles, and decide to change. Resting one day a week is not only a Biblical mandate, but is absolutely necessary for our health and longevity. One of the greatest "silver linings" in the COVID-19 crisis, is recovering the secret power of slowing down our pace a bit and spending more "down time" with Him.

But what if your loss has been so great, so devastating, you can't see any silver-linings, and your faith is at an all-time low? This is a tough one. We know all God's promises are true... are "Yes" and "Amen"; that no weapon formed against you will prosper; no plague shall come nigh your dwelling. But it's clear that bad things do sometimes happen to good people... to God's people. Jesus warned us that in this world we will still have tribulation. But our confidence is that He has overcome the world. We may experience pain and loss here, but we will ultimately triumph through unwavering faith in Him. He has won the victory for us at the Cross. When we endure through faith, we are strengthened by our trials.

Even for the strongest Christian, crisis can cause us to question our relationship with God and ask, *if God really loved me, how could He let this happen to me*? The truth is that God loves us regardless of the circumstances we face. The Bible gives us many examples of men and women who were greatly loved and used by God, and yet still faced times of crisis, pain and loss. So if a "problem free" life is not the answer, how do we actually know He loves us?

The last lesson we'll look at is probably the best one to take forward in to the next crisis. Clearly, life deals everyone lemons some of the time, and COVID-19 was one, big honkin' lemon! People have gone through an historical event that will have repercussions for years. Most have reacted and adapted without much thinking, trying to cope using their own strength. But the fact is, our strength is insufficient when faced with a crisis as large as COVID-19. We must turn to the Word of God for insight in how to turn life's lemons into lemonade.

That takes me back to Romans 8:28, and God's promise... that no matter how big your crisis is, He is even bigger. He is able to turn ALL THINGS around for your good, if you will place your faith and trust in Him. Apply these lessons to your life today, and I am confident you will crush your next crisis!

LESSON TWO
Things Can Change Suddenly

Now as they led Him away, they laid hold of a certain man, Simon a Cyrenian, who was coming from the country, and on him they laid the cross that he might bear it after Jesus. There were also two others, criminals, led with Him to be put to death. And when they had come to the place called Calvary, there they crucified Him, and the criminals, one on the right hand and the other on the left. Then Jesus said, "Father, forgive them, for they do not know what they do."
Luke 23:26, 32-34 NKJV

Is there any message needed more in a moment of crisis than the hope-filled message of the cross? The message that God loves us so much that He'd do anything to rescue us? The Apostle Paul reminded us of this when he said:

...but we preach Christ crucified, to the Jews a stumbling block and to the Greeks foolishness, but to those who are called, both Jews and Greeks, Christ the power of God and the wisdom of God.
1 Corinthians 1:23 NKJV

Just a few short days prior to the crucifixion, Jesus was being cheered by throngs of people as He made His triumphant entry into Jerusalem on a donkey. They laid palm branches before Him and hailed Him as their king. The pomp and circumstance that surrounded Him was akin to New Year's Eve celebrations in Times Square. You might even say, Jesus was the flavor of the day.

But in an instant, the cheers of jubilee from this crowd turned into jeers of "Crucify Him!" One moment, He is being hailed as King of the Jews, and the next, He is mocked with the same title. The cross of Jesus Christ reminds us that things in life can change in an instant.

Crisis comes out of nowhere... just like we experienced with COVID-19. One moment the stock market was at an all time high, the next moment it took the biggest dip in history. One moment, the unemployment rate was at an historic low, the next moment, 30 million people lost their jobs. One moment, the whole economy was soaring, the next moment, it was teetering on a second Great Depression. One moment, we were eating and drinking and living life large and the next moment... standing as a nation at death's door.

The cross of Christ reminds us that things in life can change suddenly.

This life is but a vapor, here today and gone tomorrow... symbolized by a dash between the dates on a tombstone. It reminds us that the things we put our trust in and the things we value most in this life, actually mean nothing in light of eternity.

In fact, what matters most is what stands between this life and the next... a great divide that separates us from God. And it's the cross that bridges this great divide and makes a way for us to get to the other side... to God.

God Loves Us

The cross of Christ represents the love and mercy of the Father, so much that it cost His son His life. Why else would Jesus go to the cross? What did He personally have to gain?

Why would He leave the tranquility of heaven for the torture of crucifixion? Why would the all-powerful God of heaven and Creator of the universe condescend to such punishment at the hands of mere men? Why would He who holds the world in His hands, allow His hands to be nailed to a tree?

Why would He whose words caused the world to come into being, refrain from using those same words to summon legions of angels to come to His rescue?

Why didn't He fight back?

Why did He remain silent as a lamb before His shearers?

Why did He go quietly as a sheep before the slaughter? Why?

What else could it be but love?

Not just any love, but a love undeserved, a love unearned, a love that often goes unrequited by men... not based on the actions of the recipient, but wholly based on the virtue of the Giver.

A love spoken of by the Apostle John when He said:

In this is love, not that we loved God, but that He loved us and sent His Son to be the propitiation for our sins. **1 John 4:10 NKJV**

... and described by the Apostle Paul:

But God demonstrates His own love toward us, in that while we were still sinners, Christ died for us. **Romans 5:8 NKJV**

Billy Graham answered the question of "why" when he said:

There He hung suspended between heaven and earth having suffered unspeakably. The spikes never held Him there; it was the chords of love that bound tighter than any nails men could mold. But God commended His great love for us even when we were still sinners in that Christ suffered for us.

But the physical suffering of Jesus Christ was not the real suffering. Many men before Him had died; others had hung on the cross longer than He did. Many men had become martyrs. The awful suffering of Jesus Christ was His spiritual death. He reached the final issue of sin, fathomed the deepest sorrow when He cried, "My God, My God, why hast Thou forsaken Me?" This cry was proof that Christ having become sin for us died physically (and spiritually) and with it having lost all sense of the Father's presence at that moment in time.

He who knew no sin was made sin for us that we might become the righteous of God in Christ Jesus. On the cross He was made sin. He was God forsaken. Because He knew no sin there is a value beyond comprehension in the penalty He bore, a penalty He did not need for Himself. How it was accomplished in the depth of the darkness man will never know.

I know one thing – He bore my sins in His body on that tree. He hung where I should have hung. The pains of hell that were my portion were heaped up on Him and I am able to go to heaven and merit that which is not my own but is His by every right!

The cross tells me that God loves me, and oh, how this world needs to understand that, especially during times of crisis.

He's Not Punishing Us

Many people have suggested that COVID-19 was sent as God's punishment on the world for sin, to which I point my fellow brothers and sisters to the cross of Jesus Christ. If there was ever a time for God to pour out punishment on mankind, it would have been at the time of the cross.

Indeed, prior to the cross Jesus was betrayed by His close friend for money, and unjustly arrested by Roman soldiers. He was ruthlessly interrogated by the Jewish High Priest; tried in a kangaroo court and found guilty with falsified evidence; abandoned by His dearest friend Peter; beaten by soldiers without justification; interrogated by Pontius Pilate; tortured by a Roman whip and condemned to death.

He was mocked by soldiers and dressed up with a fake royal robe and a king's crown made out of thorns. He was ordered to carry His own cross up to Golgotha, the place of execution.

He was stripped of His robe and exposed to shame before the crowds that jeered Him as He passed. He was stretched out on the beams and His hands and feet were nailed by six-inch iron spikes. He was lifted up and suspended between two wicked men, until He took His last breath.

If there was ever a time for God to pour out His punishment on humanity... that would have been the time.

But instead of screaming out in vengeance, His first words from the cross were puzzling. They are recorded in the text, *"Father, forgive them, for they do not know what they do."*

That's not what I would have said. In fact, you would have had to bleep out what I would have said!

But that's what He said.

And what He said is a message from the cross for this moment in history, and for every time crisis surrounds us... that God is not punishing us! We must never forget that God loves us and will rescue and forgive us!

Don't believe me? Remember what Scripture tells us:

For God was in Christ, reconciling the world to Himself, no longer counting people's sins against them. **2 Corinthians 5:19 NLT**

Can I Illustrate this for you? Maybe you saw the movie about Mr. Rogers called, "A Beautiful Day in the Neighborhood." In the movie, Mr. Rogers introduces his audience to his friends by showing them a picture board with a few of his friends on it. There was Mr. McFeely, King Friday, Daniel the Tiger, Lady Elaine... and his friend Lloyd.

And when he shows the picture of Lloyd, he says: "This is my friend Lloyd. He is having a hard time forgiving now." His father walked out on him, his sister and his dying mother. Eventually Lloyd and his sister had to put their mother to rest, all by themselves. As a result Lloyd had built up a tremendous amount of bitterness, anger and unforgiveness toward his father. The movie chronicles Lloyd's journey to forgiving his father... with Mr. Roger's help.

As inspirational as that is, it doesn't hold a candle to my friend and Savior Jesus. Unlike Lloyd, He is not having a hard time forgiving now. Matter of fact, when He should have punished us, He prayed for us. When He should have shouted, "Father, repay them," He prayed, "Father, forgive them."

And here is the thing about my friend and Savior Jesus... the prayer He prayed was not just for them – it was for us as well.

For them, He prayed, "Father forgive them for they know not what they do." But for us, the prayer would go something like this... "Father, forgive them, even though they often know what they do!"

Do you understand the wonderful message of the cross? It's greater than simply, God is not punishing us, but it's that God is forever waiting and wanting to forgive us! And the forgiveness my friend and Savior Jesus offers does not come with an expiration date.

He prayed that prayer from the cross and today still, the word of God tells us that He ever lives to make intercession for us. He is still offering forgiveness in place of punishment. In fact, it is Heaven's central message.

It's like the old song says:

There is a fountain filled with blood that flows from Emmanuel's veins, and sinners plunged beneath that flood lose all their guilty stains.

We Have a Choice

And when they had come to the place called Calvary, there they crucified Him, and the criminals, one on the right hand and the other on the left. **Luke 23:33 NKJV**

We know from later on in the text that one thief denied who Jesus was and what He was offering. The other thief accepted who He was and what He was offering. He accepted that He was the Savior of the world who had come, not to punish us, but to grant us forgiveness for our sins.

Jesus said to him, "You will be with Me in paradise."

These two thieves represent the only two choices we have in this life regarding who Jesus is and what He came to offer us.

We can't earn forgiveness. The Law of Moses taught us that; we are too imperfect. No matter how hard we may try, we will always fall short. God knew that ... and so He doesn't ask us to earn it, but rather, He asks us to choose it... to choose life.

But in order to be forgiven we must *choose* to repent of our sins and put our faith in Christ as our Savior. We need to choose to draw near to God, because the fact is, we desperately need Him... especially in a crisis!

This first lesson we learned from the COVID-19 experience was that things can change suddenly. Our lives are affected by the circumstances around us; but the cross of Jesus Christ reminds us that God will spare no expense to save us and protect us. When we put our trust and faith in Him, we can face any crisis knowing that He will be in it with us.

LESSON THREE
Check Your Lens

For we walk by faith, not by sight. **2 Corinthians 5:7 NKJV**

The world views everything around it through the lens of fear: from climate change to murder hornets and most recently, COVID-19. This lens is used to determine how to deal with hospitals, governmental policies, resource allocation, how to repair the economy, what safety practices need to remain in place and for how long, how to protect life, who is most vulnerable... and the list goes on.

We pray that those decision-makers that look through that lens can gain wisdom to make the wisest decisions possible, because they affect all of us.

Ultimately though, there is a greater lens, a better lens... a lens of hope and healing to look through. It's called the lens of faith, and indeed, it is a superior lens.

So often when we Christians talk about faith we talk about it like it's some kind of lever. We look at faith in light of powerful stories in Scripture, like when Jesus said to two blind men in Matthew 9:29, as He touched their eyes and said, *"According to your faith let it be to you."* Or when Jesus said to Jairus in Mark 5:36, after discovering that his daughter had died, *"Do not be afraid; only believe."* Or perhaps, we look at faith in light of what James, the half-brother of Jesus, wrote in the first chapter of James, *"If any of you lacks wisdom, let him ask of God, who gives to all liberally and without reproach, and it will be given to him. But let him ask in faith, with no doubting, for he who doubts is like a wave of the sea driven and tossed by the wind. For let not that man suppose that he will receive anything from the Lord; he is a double-minded man, unstable in all his ways." **James 1:5-8 NKJV**

When we look at faith in light of these and many other verses, we could come away with a misunderstanding that faith is simply a "lever" that we pull in moments of need which allows us to receive what God already wants for us. Sadly, we attempt to pull that lever like a slot machine in Las Vegas, hoping we hit triple sevens in heaven and receive His outpouring of blessings like a jackpot.

Understand that, indeed, the Scripture teaches that faith is an absolute requirement in receiving anything from the Lord. Hebrews 11:6 reminds us *"But without faith it is impossible to please Him, for he who comes to God must believe that He is, and that He is a rewarder of those who diligently seek Him."*

That means God is a rewarder, not a life wrecker. We must have faith when it comes to receiving from God. Faith is not a "maybe," it's a "must." When it comes down to it, faith is one of the power twins in salvation.

For by grace you have been saved through faith, and that not of yourselves; it is the gift of God, not of works, lest anyone should boast. ***Ephesians 2:8-9 NKJV***

Everything that is good comes from God, comes by grace and comes through faith. To be sure, faith is the pathway through which God's promises of grace manifest themselves in our lives.

Grace is the reason, and faith is the road. Grace (*God's Riches At Christ's Expense*) makes all of God's goodness toward us possible. Faith (*Father's Assurance In The Heart*) is the pathway by which God's promises travel from heaven to our earth.

Be that as it may, there is a better way to think of faith than as a lever that we pull which produces a promised result. That better way is to see faith as a lens... a way that helps us to see more clearly. It is a way that helps us comprehend and make sense out of what is confusing, that helps us to see Christ even in the midst of crisis... a way that helps us to see that even when we can't trace God's hand, we can trust His heart!

Faith is the way that even though we can't see Him, we know that He's working for our good in every situation we face. He never stops working. Faith helps you to see the invisible hand of God in the midst of seemingly impossible circumstances. Just like the lenses of a pair of glasses help correct the refraction error that blurs your vision by letting in light, the lens of faith lets in the light of heaven so you can make sense of what's happening on earth.

Faith is not a lever that sometimes hits and sometimes misses; it is a lens that is always available to guide us through the darkness.

Are you looking at your crisis through the lens of faith or the lens of fear? It makes all the difference in the world. Indeed, every Bible hero looked at life through the lens of faith.

Elisha, the great prophet of God and his servant were surrounded by a confederate of enemy armies. The servant was anxious and worried and he frantically said to Elisha, "What are we going to do?!" Death looked imminent; the situation looked ominous... but instead of fear, Elisha prayed.

*So he answered, "Do not fear, for those who are with us are more than those who are with them." And Elisha prayed, and said, "Lord, I pray, open his eyes that he may see." Then the Lord opened the eyes of the young man, and he saw. And behold, the mountain was full of horses and chariots of fire all around Elisha. **2 Kings 6:16 -17 NKJV***

The servant was panicking, but Elisha was in perfect peace. Elisha was looking at the crisis through the lens of faith.

In another example, Elijah (Elisha's mentor), had sent his servant out in the midst of a drought to check for any sign of rain. The servant came back after checking seven different times without success, and said:

"There is a cloud, as small as a man's hand, rising out of the sea!" ***1 Kings 18:44 NKJV***

And Elijah said, "Go up, say to Ahab, 'Prepare your chariot, and go down before the rain stops you.'"

The servant probably thought Elijah was crazy. *Didn't he hear me say there was nothing in the sky but a cloud the size of a man's hand?* Elijah heard him correctly, but what he heard was filtered through the lens of faith and therefore he saw the situation differently. He saw a great abundance of rain coming to end the drought in the land.

How about Abraham, the father of our faith? God told him to offer up his promised son, Isaac, as a sacrifice. So Abraham and Isaac travel up the mountain. Isaac sees the wood, sees the fire, sees the altar, and asks Dad... *but where is the sacrifice?* And Abraham replies:

"My son, God will provide for Himself the lamb for a burnt offering." **Genesis 22:8 NKJV**

Abraham was looking at his life during the most difficult circumstance, not through the lens of what "is", but through the lens of faith. And God rewarded him for it.

How about the account of Shadrach, Meshach and Abednego? Their captor, the Babylonian king Nebuchadnezzar declared himself a god, and said to them, "If you don't bow down before me, I'm going to throw you into a burning, fiery furnace!"

They said, "Oh no! We ain't bowing and if you do throw us in, we want you to know,

...our God whom we serve is able to deliver us from the burning fiery furnace, and He will deliver us from your hand, O king. **Daniel 3:17 NKJV**

They looked at their crisis through the lens of faith.

Faith is not a lever that we pull, it's a lens that we look through that enables us to be at peace in the midst of pandemics; to expect big things despite little evidence; to trust God in times of trouble, and make sense out of suffering. Faith enables us to stay strong despite circumstances that ought to make us crumble. It allows us to maintain a sound mind in a scary world and to have hope in the face of despair. Ultimately, faith provides protection, though we may be surrounded by problems.

Faith is a superior lens to the lens of fear. It's not that we are ignorant optimists, but rather that we've been to the Heavenly Optometrist. It's not that we ignore what is, it's that we have a greater confidence in the One who holds our life in His hands. It's not that we are immune to what is around us, it's that we have evidence of Who surrounds us. Look with the eyes of faith!

But if we are not careful, we might suppose that only Bible greats naturally look through the lens of faith—as if some people have a "faith gene" and some don't. Truth is, the "greats" only become great because they choose to look through the lens of faith during the midst of their crisis.

When you read the story in Scripture of the twelve spies sent to the Promised Land, you find that the twelve were all cut from the same cloth. That is, each one was the best that their respective tribe had to offer. They each had been raised with the same opportunities and had experienced the same privileges. And they went into the Promised Land together and saw the same thing... a blessed land.

As the Scripture puts it, it was a land "flowing with milk and honey." (Picture Willy Wonka's chocolate factory!) All twelve spies saw that the land had produce that looked like it was pumped with steroids – with grapes that were as big as basketballs...and they all saw the giants who lived in the land.

These giants were men of great stature, called "sons of Anak," as the Bible describes them. Many

Bible scholars believe these people to be the offspring between fallen angels and human women, as described in Genesis 6. (Think big, bad, ugly, protruding foreheads, abnormal pituitary gland-looking giants!)

But when these twelve men, the "best of the best" come back from spying out the Promised Land, ten of them say:

"We went to the land where you sent us. It truly flows with milk and honey, and this is its fruit. Nevertheless the people who dwell in the land are strong; the cities are fortified and very large; moreover we saw the descendants of Anak there. The Amalekites dwell in the land of the South; the Hittites, the Jebusites, and the Amorites dwell in the mountains; and the Canaanites dwell by the sea and along the banks of the Jordan."

..."We are not able to go up against the people, for they are stronger than we." And they gave the children of Israel a bad report of the land which they had spied out, saying, "The land through which we have gone as spies is a land that devours its inhabitants, and all the people whom we saw in it are men of great stature. There we saw the giants (the descendants of Anak came from the

*giants); and we were like grasshoppers in our own sight, and so we were in their sight." **Numbers 13:27-29, 31-33 NKJV***

Ten of the twelve men, or 83.33%, chose to see life through the lens of circumstances and apparent failure. Ten of them **chose** to look at life through a losing lens!

But there were two who chose to look at life through the lens of God, the lens of possibilities... the lens of faith.

*Then Caleb quieted the people before Moses, and said, "Let us go up at once and take possession, for we are well able to overcome it." **Numbers 13:30 NKJV***

Here, two sets of people get exposed to the same thing:

- Same promised land
- Same giants
- Same grapes
- Same instructions

But, some chose to see and respond with the lens of faith, and the others chose the lens of circumstances and fear. So what is the take away? Looking through the lens of faith is a choice we all must make in any situation. There is no "faith gene." It's not automatic, but rather it requires you to choose.

> *I call heaven and earth as witnesses today against you, that I have set before you life and death, blessing and cursing; therefore choose life, that both you and your descendants may live; ...*
> **Deuteronomy 30:19 NKJV**

Choosing the lens of faith is choosing life; any other lens is inferior and produces bondage, not freedom. Sometimes you can't stop what happens to you, but the lens of faith keeps the life of God flowing through you!

Famous psychologist and World War II Nazi concentration camp survivor, Viktor Frankle, in his book, *Man's Search for Meaning,* speaks of mastering the art of living even in the worst conditions possible. In recounting his experience, he did not deny the reality of the grimness of his situation in the camps, but he said, "I envisioned myself lecturing on the lessons I was learning in the concentration camp after my release." He went on to famously say, "The last of all human freedoms is to choose one's attitude in any given set of circumstances."

You can choose to look at life and every circumstance through the lens of faith! Here are a few tips to help you!

Watch What You Say

Notice the difference between what Caleb and Joshua said, and what the other ten spies said. Caleb and Joshua said, "We are well able to overcome it." However, the other ten said "The land is strong, the cities are fortified and very large, the giants are big and we are grasshoppers." Those that spoke words filled with faith were able to look at life through the lens of faith, and those that spoke "facts" were only able to see failure.

What you say has a profound effect over the lens that you choose to look through. Don't deny the facts, but do speak by faith. So choose to declare Psalm 91 over your life and over the life of your loved ones. Declare every morning that you dwell in the secret place of the Most High and abide under the shadow and covering of the Almighty. Agree with Him that God is your refuge and your fortress, in Him you will trust. Confess out loud that He will deliver you from harm, and that no evil shall befall you, nor any plague come near your house. Declare with the psalmist that He will give His angels charge over you, and will answer you when you call on Him in prayer. Never forget He will be with you in trouble, and will deliver you. Declare that all of God's promises toward you are "Yes" and "Amen!"

Speak faith... have faith! Speak life... have life! Believe He is FOR YOU, not AGAINST YOU, and you will be able to look at every situation through the lens of faith!

Watch What You See

The Scripture says that two of the spies carried one of these massive clusters of grapes back from the Promised Land to the camp of Israel. It never states who those two men were, but I would bet the ranch that it was Caleb and Joshua!

When everyone else had their eyes fixed on the size of the giants around them, Caleb and Joshua had their eyes fixed on the grapes before them.

In the midst of any crisis like COVID-19, fix your focus on what's good, not on the "giants" of the situation. That means...

- Stop watching the death toll numbers
- Stop watching the stock market ticker
- Stop allowing the nightly news to fill you with fear
- Go around your house and remember all your blessings
- Remember every promise God has already fulfilled in your life
- Think about things that are good, pure, and lovely
- Be like Jesus, who fixed His eyes on what was good in the middle of a crisis

*...who for the joy that was set before Him endured the cross, despising the shame, and has sat down at the right hand of the throne of God. **Hebrews 12:2 NKJV***

Jesus fixed His focus on His joy: you and me!

He kept looking at the good things before Him, salvation for mankind, that incredible plan for redemption. That's how He endured the cross.

Joshua and Caleb looked at the reward of the grapes, while Jesus looked at us. We also need to be careful what we look at if we are going to look through the right lens, the lens of faith. It seems obvious, but what you pay attention to determines what lens you look through.

Isn't that what happened to Peter?

Remember the account of Jesus coming to the disciples in the middle of a storm, walking on the sea? At first, the disciples thought He was a ghost and were terrified. Then Peter boldly said, "Lord if it's You, bid me to come to you." Jesus said "Come," and Peter stepped out of the boat and began walking on the water! Amazing!

But then the Scripture says:

*But when he saw that the wind was boisterous, he was afraid; and beginning to sink he cried out, saying, "Lord, save me!" **Matthew 4:30 NKJV***

In other words, when Peter took his eyes off of the Author and Finisher of his faith (Jesus), and focused instead on the "facts" that surrounded him (the storm and waves), he lost faith and began to sink.

Like Peter, we also need to watch what we pay attention to when we are going through life's storms, so that we can keep looking through the lens of faith.

Watch What You Hear

Caleb and Joshua agreed with what God said. They said, "We are able." They declared, "God is with us." On multiple occasions, they cut short those that were speaking about how bad the situation in the Promised Land was, and reminded them of what God had promised. Every time these faithful men spoke up and encouraged the people to believe God, they were actually coaching them about what it takes to intentionally "choose" to look through the lens of faith, and what it means to stay in agreement with the Word of God. That is, it's important to watch what you hear.

So then faith comes by hearing, and hearing by the word of God. **Romans 10:17 NKJV**

What does that mean? Generally, what you hear most often will determine what you will believe and have faith in. Understanding that is so important today. If you must watch the news to know what's going on remember to "hear" the Word of God on the matter!

Saturate your mind with the Word of God. Saturate your soul and your spirit, because it's medicine for your mind and body, and light to your lens.

My son, give attention to my words; Incline your ear to my sayings. Do not let them depart from your eyes; Keep them in the midst of your heart; For they are life to those who find them, And health to all their flesh. **Proverbs 4:20-22 NKJV**

Do not forget God's Word! In times of crisis, remember His promises:

"For I know the plans I have for you," declares the Lord, "plans to prosper you and not to harm you, plans to give you hope and a future. **Jeremiah 29:11 NIV**

Weeping may endure for a night, But joy comes in the morning. **Psalm 30:5 NKJV**

To console those who mourn in Zion, to give them beauty for ashes, the oil of joy for mourning... **Isaiah 61:3 NKJV**

Then He who sat on the throne said, "Behold, I make all things new." **Revelation 21:5 NKJV**

And we know that all things work together for good to those who love God, to those who are the called according to His purpose. **Romans 8:28 NKJV**

Choose the right life lens... the lens of faith. You will be happy that you did!

Protection from "Infection"

After the spies came back and shared their bad report with the rest of the congregation, the next verse says:

> *So all the congregation lifted up their voices and cried, and the people wept that night.* **Numbers 14:1 NKJV**

They did not practice safe "social distancing" from absolutely toxic and infectious information! As a result, most of Israel got infected with the virus of worry, anxiety and fear... and it crippled them.

It's so important to remember when a crisis hits us (like it did with COVID-19), we must "social distance" from worry, anxiety and fear, which are simply the tools of the devil! The best way to do that is by taking up the "shield of faith." Listen to what the Scripture says in Ephesians 6:

...above all, taking the shield of faith with which you will be able to quench all the fiery darts of the wicked one. **Ephesians 6:16 NKJV**

Like a face mask that helps prevent the spread of disease, the "shield of faith" prevents the infection of your mind with toxic thoughts, the fiery darts the enemy tries to throw our way... including worry and fear. Or mind games.

In fact, the enemy wants to disrupt our lives with darts to the mind that cripple us. But that's exactly where the lens of faith comes in handy!

The lens of faith provides us with protection from this kind of mental infection, and Satan's ultimate battle is a battle for your mind. Looking at life through the lens of faith enables you to win that battle, and ultimately enables you to find the good in the midst of bad.

There is a joke that has gone around recently that demonstrates this perfectly:

There once was a family with two young boys. One of the boys was a terrible pessimist; the other was an incessant optimist. The parents were getting worried because each son's personality was so extreme. The father said, "We need to do something to break them out of their molds."

So on Christmas morning, the parents filled up the pessimist's bedroom with dozens and dozens of brand new toys, and they filled up the optimist's room with horse manure... hoping this would change their attitudes.

Well, after the children were in their rooms for a couple of hours, the pessimist came out, and the father asked, "Did you play with your new toys?"

The pessimist moaned, "Nah, I never even opened the packages. I was afraid that if I touched them, they'd just break, and I'd be disappointed."

Then the optimist came bounding out of his room that had been filled with horse manure, and he was all smiles. His dad said, "Why are you so happy?"

The little boy smiled and said, "I just know that if I keep digging long enough, I'm going to find a pony!"

Life isn't always good and doesn't always turn out the way we hope, but when we look through the lens of faith, it helps us find the good despite the bad.

I believe it was John Ortberg who observed,

Optimism, in the Biblical sense, is not about hyping myself into believing that everything is going to turn out the way I want it. And it is, in particular, not the idea that I can have whatever job will make me feel successful and whatever house I think would be comfortable to me and accumulate as much money as I want to accumulate and get married to somebody who I think is real attractive to me and have as much fun and pleasure and power and status and prestige in life as I want to, as long as I keep real positive and am able to visualize it and so on. (that's the lever of faith) That's not what it's about.

It is the confident expectation that an all-powerful God is at work, even in this fallen world, to redeem it and to bring good out of it. And it's not just that. It's not just that I believe that there is a God out there. It is also the confident expectation that this same good, powerful God is intimately aware of and deeply concerned about my life, my future, and the role He wants me to play in His work in this world.

In the Bible, Joseph was betrayed by his older brothers, sold into slavery, and spent time in prison because of their jealousy. Years later, after he had become Prime Minister over Egypt, Joseph had the opportunity to take revenge on his brothers when they came to buy grain during a famine. When the brothers discovered the true identity of this powerful ruler, they were shaking in their boots! But Joseph chose to view his circumstances through the lens of faith. Listen to what he said to them:

"Don't be afraid. Am I in the place of God? You intended to harm me, but God intended it for good to accomplish what is now being done, the saving of many lives. **Genesis 50:19-20 NIV**

How did Joseph come to that conclusion... given the backdrop of years of pain, betrayal, and terrible circumstances? He *chose* to look at his life through the lens of faith, and that attitude eventually led him to rule as administrator over the most powerful empire of his day.

We can also learn from the account of Esther, an orphaned girl, whose land was invaded, and people taken into captivity by the Persians. She was again marginalized by being forced to enter a "beauty contest" to become the Persian King's arm candy.

Through a series of divinely orchestrated events, Esther became queen of Persia. In time, an enemy of the Jewish people gained the King's confidence and persuaded him to have the Jewish captives destroyed. Esther's true identity as a Jewess had not been known, and Esther was given the opportunity to use her position to save her people from this mass execution. But Esther had to *choose* to look at her situation through the lens of faith, because to approach the King with her request, without first being summoned, meant putting her life at great risk. Esther's Uncle Mordecai encouraged her to face her fear with faith, and he reminds her of the power of God over her circumstances:

"And who knows but that you have come to your royal position for such a time as this?" **Esther 4:14 NKJV**

How could Esther view her life's journey like that, in light of all the terrible things she had endured that led up to that moment of crisis? She looked through the lens of faith.

Then there's the story of young David, who was an overlooked shepherd boy whose own father didn't think enough of him to consider him to be "king material" when the prophet Samuel came to town. But one day, his father sent David on an errand to bring his older brothers some pizza on the battlefield. (Pizza... you know... bread and cheese!)

During the battle, the entire army of Israel was stricken with fear, and no one wanted to go out to face the enemy's champion, a giant named Goliath. They looked at him through the lens of fear, and said "This warrior is too big to defeat." David, however, looked through the lens of faith and said, "I'll go, because he's just too big to miss with my sling and stone!"

How was David able to look at his circumstances and say, "God will deliver this uncircumcised Philistine into my hands," when everyone else said it was impossible? He believed God and looked at his circumstances, his giant, through the lens of faith.

One final example...

A Jewish exile named Naomi had lost her husband and both her sons while living in a foreign land, and thereafter, she decided to return to her homeland of Israel. However, one of her daughters-in-law, a woman named Ruth, refused to leave her side. She travelled with Naomi back to Israel, and began following some local grain harvesters to pick up loose grain to feed herself and her mother-in-law, Naomi.

While she was working one day, Boaz, the rich owner of the field took notice of her. She eventually married him and owned that very field! Even more amazing was that God gave her a son who was directly in the lineage of Jesus, the Messiah.

When Naomi (whose life had, at one time, seemed hopeless), held that little boy in her arms, the women of her town said to her:

"Praise be to the Lord, who this day has not left you without a guardian-redeemer. May he become famous throughout Israel! He will renew your life and sustain you in your old age. For your daughter-in-law, who loves you and who is better to you than seven sons, has given him birth." **Ruth 4:14 NIV**

Naomi held the child and received their words with great joy. But how did she praise God against the backdrop of such grief, fear and anxiety from all those tragedies she had faced in her life? She *chose* to view them through the lens of faith.

This lens is available for you and me to look through as well. It enables us to see what is invisible to others. It enables us to overcome life's heartaches and still hold onto a joy unspeakable and full of glory, deep within our souls.

It causes a peace that passes all understanding to be our portion, and bellows within the chambers of our hearts despite the circumstances that surround us. It helps us to say, regardless of what surrounds us... it is well with my soul.

The lens of faith lights our way.

It helps us to see the good hand of God against the backdrop of life's evil and pain. It gives us an eternal assurance that all things are working together for the good, even when good is being masked by the epitome of evil. It lifts our eyes to the hills from whence comes our help.

The lens of faith says, what the enemy meant for evil against me, God will turn around and use for good. You can declare that God will use that very thing to make me stronger. It's better than a magnifying glass, it's superior to a set of glasses, and it sees further than the most powerful telescope. It is the lens of faith!

And my prayer is that you too will look through it to face any crisis:

- Look through it if you're sick
- Look through it if you've lost your job
- Look through it if you're struggling to put groceries on the table
- Look through it if you lost a loved one
- Look through it if you have no hope left
- Look through it if you need help

- Look through it you've lost hope
- Look through if you are in despair
- Look through it when you're up and when you're down

So what COVID-19 taught us in this lesson is that we should never view life's circumstances the way the world does... through the lens of fear, rather than faith. Our worldview is better, and leads to a better outcome in the end, we consistently watch what we see, hear and say about it.

No matter what comes your way, look at it through the lens of faith, and you will find Christ in the midst of crisis, the Lord of Glory in the midst of worry... the Savior, Jesus Christ in the midst of life's storms. Always look through the lens of faith!

LESSON FOUR
Turn Fear into Faith

He who dwells in the secret place of the Most High Shall abide under the shadow of the Almighty. I will say of the LORD, "He is my refuge and my fortress; My God, in Him I will trust." Surely He shall deliver you from the snare of the fowler And from the perilous pestilence. He shall cover you with His feathers, And under His wings you shall take refuge; His truth shall be your shield and buckler. You shall not be afraid of the terror by night, Nor of the arrow that flies by day, Nor of the pestilence that walks in darkness, Nor of the destruction that lays waste at noonday. A thousand may fall at your side, And ten thousand at your right hand; But it shall not come near you. Only with your eyes shall you look, And see the reward of the wicked. Because you have made the LORD, who is my refuge, Even the Most High, your dwelling place, No evil shall befall you, Nor shall any plague come near your dwelling; For He shall give His angels charge over you, To keep you in all your ways. In their hands they shall bear you up, Lest you dash your foot against a stone. You shall tread upon the lion and the cobra, The young lion and the serpent you shall trample underfoot." Because he has set his love upon Me, therefore I will deliver him; I will set him on high, because he has known My name. He shall call upon Me, and I will answer him; I will be with him in trouble; I will deliver *him and honor him. With long life I will satisfy him, And show him My salvation." **Psalm 91 NKJV***

Those are some mighty promises to hold onto when facing a crisis. But, do you believe them? Do you really believe the promises of the Word of God? It's easy to believe when everything is going right, isn't it?

It's easy to believe the Lord is your provider when your bank account is full. It's not as easy when there's more month at the end of your money. It's easy to believe that God is your healer when you are young and healthy, but what about when things go wrong with your body... is God still your healer?

Do we *believe* the Word of God? Do we believe that He is the same, yesterday, today and forever? Do we believe that God is greater than anything the enemy may throw at us? Do we really believe the Word of the Lord?

In Psalm 91, there are several broad maladies of life that God promises to protect us from:

- shelter from the snares or traps of life
- shelter from pestilence or deadly misfortune
- shelter from terror or sudden death
- shelter from destruction or ruin
- shelter from evil or sin, and exceedingly heavy grief
- shelter from plagues (including pandemics!)
- shelter from trouble, adversity and distress

This is not to say that these are the only things that are promised to us. Rather, God promises that His protections are broad and He is faithful to protect His people from whatever the world can throw at us. So pray Psalm 91 over your life! It's supernatural protection!

However, this is not to say that faith and wisdom are mutually exclusive. You should not operate in faith at the exclusion of wisdom. Faith and wisdom go hand in hand... even more, it's evident that to stay in faith, you must walk in wisdom.

*My brethren, count it all joy when you fall into various trials, knowing that the testing of your faith produces patience. But let patience have its perfect work, that you may be perfect and complete, lacking nothing. If any of you lacks wisdom, let him ask of God, who gives to all liberally and without reproach, and it will be given to him. But let him ask in faith, with no doubting, for he who doubts is like a wave of the sea driven and tossed by the wind. For let not that man suppose that he will receive anything from the Lord; he is a double-minded man, unstable in all his ways. **James 1:1-8 NKJV**

Faith. Wisdom. Faith. They work together. We control what we can, and God promises to protect us from what we can't... and these include:

DWELLING Power

He who dwells in the secret place of the Most High shall abide under the shadow of the Almighty. **Psalm 91:1 NKJV**

Quite often, we think of this passage as a performance-based promise, available only to those saints who pray for two hours every day. But if that were true it would disqualify 99.9999% of the Church! It's not a performance-based promise, but a position-based promise.

If you have confessed Jesus Christ as Lord over your life, when God looks at you... He sees Jesus! No strings attached. You are saved, forgiven and protected.

*For you died, and your life is hidden with Christ in God. **Colossians 3:3 NKJV***

That means, you died, and you now abide in Christ! Look again...

*Whoever confesses that Jesus is the Son of God, God abides in him, and he in God. **1 John 4:15 NKJV***

You abide in God if you confess Jesus Christ. Does that say ANYTHING about your perfect performance as a Christian? No. It is a position in Christ-based promise! The protection of God covers His people.

But, do you have to have faith for it? The Bible says, "My people perish for lack of knowledge" (Hosea 4:6), not lack of performance. We must anchor our faith to our identity in Christ, not to our performance. If you anchor to anything but your position in Christ, your faith will shake.

SAYING Power

I will say of the LORD, "He is my refuge and my fortress; My God, in Him I will trust." **Psalm 91:2 NKJV**

Watch what you say. When you say things that feed fear, it will destroy your faith. When you say things that feed your faith, it destroys your fear. What are you saying?

Think of the children's story called, "The Little Engine That Could." Everybody said this little train engine was too small to pull a big load up a mountain. But he kept saying to himself... "I think I can, I think I can," and he finally succeeded.

Your words will empower your faith and destroy your fear, or they will destroy your faith and power your fear.

Fear is a spiritual force that you must overcome. It is sent by the enemy to erode the faith of God's people.

For God has not given us a spirit of fear, but of power and of love and of a sound mind. **2 Timothy 1:7 NKJV**

In everything we encounter in life there are two forces at play... the forces of darkness and the forces of God. The way we power up faith to overcome and power down fear, is to watch what you say. *I will say of the LORD, "He is my refuge and my fortress; My God, in Him I will trust!"*

"TRUTHING" Power

His truth shall be your shield and buckler. **Psalm 91:4 NKJV**

What is "truthing"? It's where we chose to base our outlook in any situation, not on the facts of life, but on the truth of Scripture.

"Facts" and "truth" are not the same. Facts can and do change all the time. Remember, it used to be a "fact" that the world was flat. Currently, it is a "fact" that there is no cure for COVID-19. But do you believe that will always be so? Facts change.

But truth doesn't change. Jesus Christ is and will always be our Healer... by His stripes we are healed. And on that cross, He bore our sins AND our sicknesses! That truth never changes! So choose to base your outlook, not on the facts of life, but on the truth of Scripture, God's Word.

LOVING Power

In this is love, not that we loved God, but that He loved us and sent His Son to be the propitiation for our sins. **1 John 4:10 NKJV**

What is love? Love is when I "do" for another person, despite whether they love me in return. True love is not motivated by reciprocation. It's unconditional and possibly unexplainable. It's like God's love for us.

Our faith cannot be hinged to our love for God which is changeable, but it can be anchored to God's love for us, which is unchangeable. Our faith is empowered to work through understanding God's love for us.

For when we are in union with Christ Jesus, neither circumcision nor the lack of it makes any difference at all; what matters is faith that works through love. **Galatians 5:6 NKJV**

My faith works because I know my Father loves me and will move heaven and earth to rescue me, to provide for me and to heal me. My Father will do it!

So what COVID-19 taught us in this lesson is that we must know the Word of God to trust the protection of God over us during a crisis. If we're honest, the forced shut down actually forced many Christians to open their Bibles for the first time in a long while and meditate on the promises of God, like those of Psalm 91. We had to rediscover how to access these promises and apply them to our lives by relearning to dwell confidently in Him, to say what He says about the matter and to activate our faith by demonstrating love towards others. All of these are important tools to have at the ready during any crisis we may face in the future!

LESSON FIVE
Get in Jesus' Boat!

On the same day, when evening had come, He said to them, "Let us cross over to the other side." Now when they had left the multitude, they took Him along in the boat as He was. And other little boats were also with Him. And a great windstorm arose, and the waves beat into the boat, so that it was already filling. But He was in the stern, asleep on a pillow. And they awoke Him and said to Him, "Teacher, do You not care that we are perishing?" Then He arose and rebuked the wind, and said to the sea, "Peace, be still!" And the wind ceased and there was a great calm. But He said to them, "Why are you so fearful? How is it that you have no faith?"
Mark 4:35-40 NKJV

Jesus had issued an order to His disciples after having an amazing day of ministry. On the same day, He had preached the Sermon on the Mount, healed a man with leprosy, spoken a word and healed the Centurion's servant, Peter's mother-in-law and "all the sick" that had been brought to Him. Jesus had just had an amazing day of ministry and He had kicked the snot out of the devil. He was physically and mentally exhausted and He then gives the order to His disciples who have just witnessed all this supernatural stuff... *Let's go to the other side.* He goes down to take a nap in the lower part of the boat, and they set sail.

All is well. The water is calm... the day perfect for sailing. The sky is blue, birds are chirping, and the disciples are riding high on the emotion of success.

Then out of nowhere... BAM! A storm of enormous size breaks out over them. The Bible call it a "squall," a massive sea storm so big it scares these professional sailors and they fear for their lives.

Let's relate this storm story to our modern life...

The economy is booming. The stock market is at an all time high. Unemployment is at an all time low. People are so blessed they are eating out at the best restaurants, going to Broadway shows. They are getting pay raises and bonuses at work. Mortgage rates are lower than ever; people are buying houses and building bigger... and BAM! Out of nowhere comes a crisis... a "squall" called COVID-19 that crippled the entire world in fear... emotionally, physically and economically.

The disciples on the boat with Jesus push the proverbial "panic button." They are filled with fear.... never a good place to be in or live in. Fear (which actually means "faithless") causes people to forget what they need to remember, because it forces them to focus on the wrong thing.

Fear causes you to focus on the storm, instead of the Savior. When that happens, you begin to sink. It's a fact... where your focus goes, the power flows. Focus on the storm and you will sink. You will take on water. Focus on the Savior and you will get to the other side.

Focus is a choice... whether you have a faith focus or a fear focus is a choice.

Finally, brethren, whatever things are true, whatever things are noble, whatever things are just, whatever things are pure, whatever things are lovely, whatever things are of good report, if there is any virtue and if there is anything praiseworthy —meditate on these things. ***Philippians 4:8 NKJV***

Think. Don't just let your mind wander, but make your thought life intentional, deliberate, and focused only on things that feed your faith and starve your fear.

When you intentionally build faith, then storms are not such a bad thing. You can actually profit from your trials with the right attitude.

My brethren, count it all joy when you fall into various trials, knowing that the testing of your faith produces patience. But let patience have its perfect work, that you may be perfect and complete, lacking nothing. **James 1:2-4 NKJV**

In other words, what the devil sends to take you out, will only make you stronger... if you keep your focus right. I can personally testify to this, that the storms that God brought me though in the past, have greatly helped to steady my faith through every new crisis. If your faith is being tested in any kind of trial, rejoice, because if you stay focused on Jesus, you will profit from the testing of your faith. But first, there are several things you need to grab onto in order to secure your faith in the storm, and avoid the trap of fear.

Do Not Forget Jesus' Word

Jesus gave His disciples a very clear direction... *let's go to the other side.* Then He went to lay down for a nap. Now, at this point in time, you would think Jesus' Word was enough... that His disciples would never doubt it. They had seen many miraculous displays of the power of His Word!

Peter should have known... after a night of unsuccessful fishing by this professional fisherman, Jesus simply said, "Cast your net on the other side of the boat," and when he did, he caught more than he had ever seen before. Jesus' Word was true!

His Word confounded the wise in the greatest sermon ever preached, what we call the Sermon on the Mount. Religious leaders of the day were dumbfounded at His wisdom. His words pierced their hearts and compelled sinners to listen. His Word was true!

Jesus met a man on the road with leprosy. No one else would touch him. He said, "If You are willing I can be made clean."

Then Jesus put out His hand and touched him, saying, "I am willing; be cleansed." Immediately his leprosy was cleansed. **Matthew 8:3 NKJV**

His Word was true!

A Roman centurion came to see Jesus and said, if you only just say the word, my servant will be healed! And Jesus said:

"Go your way; and as you have believed, so let it be done for you." And his servant was healed that same hour. **Matthew 8:13 NKJV**

His Word was true!

The same Word that the disciples saw working in power, in signs and wonders, was true! His street credibility with His disciples should have been through the roof! He said, *"Let's cross over to the other side.*" But they forgot His Word, they forgot the promise, and they focused instead on the fear.

Do not forget Jesus' Word in your crisis. No matter what storm hits, no matter how devastating it appears, remember what He has promised:

*Then the LORD said to me, "You have seen well, for I am ready to perform My word." **Jeremiah 1:12 NKJV***

*So shall My word be that goes forth from My mouth; It shall not return to Me void, But it shall accomplish what I please, And it shall prosper in the thing for which I sent it. **Isaiah 55:11 NKJV***

*For all the promises of God in Him are Yes, and in Him Amen, to the glory of God through us. **2 Corinthians 1:20 NKJV***

That means...

- No weapon formed against you will prosper
- No evil shall befall you nor any plague come near your dwelling
- He is your refuge and your fortress
- He is an ever present help in time of trouble
- All things will work together for your good
- He is the Healer of all our diseases

And you are going to get to the other side, because Jesus is in your boat! So do not forget Jesus' word!

Do Not Forget to Speak to the Storm

The disciples woke Jesus up in a panic, thinking they were about to die. After calming the storm with a word, He turned to them and said... *"How is it that you have no faith?"* Very likely He could have said to them, *You know My will in the matter... you could have... you SHOULD have spoken to the storm, yourself!*

One of the great privileges and responsibilities of the Church is the power to stand and speak to the storms of life, in the name of Jesus.

For assuredly, I say to you, whoever says to this mountain, 'Be removed and be cast into the sea,' and does not doubt in his heart, but believes that those things he says will be done, he will have whatever he says. Therefore I say to you, whatever things you ask when you pray, believe that you receive them, and you will have them. **Mark 11:23-24 NKJV**

You will also declare a thing, And it will be established for you; So light will shine on your ways. **Job 22:23 NKJV**

In order to do His will in your storm, however, you must stop speaking "about" your storm as though you are going to be destroyed by it. Instead, God wants you to speak "to" your storm in the Name of Jesus.

Speak to the storm raging over your family, over your kids, your marriage, your parents.

Speak to the storm swirling around your finances. Then Church, speak victory over every storm that God leads you to confront, for yourself and in intercession for others. Use your power in the Name of Jesus Christ to bring victory and the glory of God in every area of life.

Let's speak the words of faith and life. Let's move mountains in the Name of Jesus Christ. No more COVID-19. No more anger. No more lying. No more evil masquerading as good! With one voice, as one Church... all across this land and around the world. Do not forget to speak to the storm!

Do Not Forget Who is in Your Boat

Now when they had left the multitude, they took Him along in the boat as He was. And other little boats were also with Him. **Mark 4:36 NKJV**

...other little boats. This verse reminds us of two important things:

1. Their boat was the biggest. Really, if you're going to go through a storm, the biggest boat is

the best choice. In other words, these disciples had something to be grateful for. If you find something to be grateful for, a silver lining to the cloud, it will help you to keep your faith strong in the storm.

...in everything give thanks; for this is the will of God in Christ Jesus for you. **1 Thessalonians 5:18 NKJV**

2. Jesus was in their boat. JESUS was in their boat! That is, in fact, one of the greatest promises in all of Scripture.

... "and lo, I am with you always, even to the end of the age." **Matthew 28:20 NKJV**

Let your conduct be without covetousness; be content with such things as you have. For He Himself has said, "I will never leave you nor forsake you." **Hebrews 13:5 NKJV**

Let me give you an example of how important it is to have the right person in your boat. Take Tom Brady, the NFL quarterback, for example. In early 2020, Tom Brady became a free agent and left the New England Patriots, and landed with the Tampa Bay Buccaneers. Prior to his arrival in Florida, the Buccaneers were 50/1 to win the Super Bowl. After the arrival of Tom Brady, their odds have jumped to 15/1. Tom Brady's impact changed the odds.

If Tom Brady's presence tilted the odds in favor of the Buccaneers by being on their team, what does Jesus in our boat do to our odds in making it to the other side? Selah.

Child of God, you've got the original odds changer on your side!

- David went up against the giant, Goliath
- Daniel faced a den of hungry lions
- Shadrach, Meshach and Abednego came out of the fiery furnace alive
- Elijah faced down 850 prophets of Baal
- Gideon conquered an army of 120,000 with 300 men

He is the odds changer, and He is in Your boat! You are going to make it to the other side!

Ultimately, this lesson we learned from COVID-19 is one of the most important. We know that as Christians, we are not promised a trouble-free life. We will certainly face trials, tribulation and crises in our lifetimes. But unlike the world, we have Christ "in our boat." We have learned that no matter how massive the storm, He is with us. And as the Lord of Glory, He is the Lord over the storm. If we remember His Word, if we remember to speak to the crisis and not about the crisis, we will ride out any storm and make it to the other side!

LESSON SIX
We're Better Together

Now from the sixth hour until the ninth hour there was darkness over all the land. And about the ninth hour Jesus cried out with a loud voice, saying "Eli, Eli, lama sabachthani?" that is, "My God, My God, why have You forsaken Me?" Some of those who stood there, when they heard that, said, "This Man is calling for Elijah!" Immediately one of them ran and took a sponge, filled it with sour wine and put it on a reed, and offered it to Him to drink. The rest said, "Let Him alone; let us see if Elijah will come to save Him." And Jesus cried out again with a loud voice, and yielded up His spirit. Then, behold, the veil of the temple was torn in two from top to bottom; and the earth quaked, and the rocks were split, and the graves were opened; and many bodies of the saints who had fallen asleep were raised; and coming out of the graves after His resurrection, they went into the holy city and appeared to many. So when the centurion and those with him, who were guarding Jesus, saw the earthquake and the things that had happened, they feared greatly, saying, "Truly this was the Son of God!" Matthew 27:45-51 NKJV

The crisis we faced from COVID-19 led to the unprecedented action of politicians shutting down the global economy and forcing people into a "shelter in place" quarantine.

Even though it may have saved lives in the long run, it appears most people's patience does have a limit. To be honest, quarantine is not fun. It goes against everything that has been built into our DNA as human beings. In fact, the "social distancing" experience has made it clear just how much we need each other.

We were never meant to be alone, never meant to do life alone, never meant to work alone, love alone or live alone. We were meant for hugs and handshakes and interaction and assembling as a congregation.

Scripture says it like this:

- It is not good for man to be alone...
- Two are better than one...
- Do not forsake the assembling together...

No matter where you stand on the issue of social distancing to fight disease, the truth is there is a growing distain in public opinion for "staying distant." We are sick of being separated from our friends and loved ones, because we're made by God to be part of a community.

We were made in God's image—the same God Who has always been, and will always be, sick of being separated from you! You are the apple of His eye, a pearl of great price... the crown jewel of His creation. You are His everlasting love, the Bride of Christ, Beloved Child of the Father... a Masterpiece!

When God made the earth, He made it a paradise and placed mankind in it. He created Adam and Eve and walked with them in the garden. The God of Heaven loved to spend time with His creation. And since the day mankind rebelled against God, He has and always will be, sick of being separated from you and me. But sin entered into the heart of man and caused a separation from Him that made God "sick."

On that fateful day, God came down for one last visit, found Adam and Eve hiding, covered their nakedness with skins, and escorted them out of the garden. He directed two cherubim (angels with flaming swords), to keep guard at the entrance of the garden and prevent anyone from entering again. He had to keep them out of the garden lest they eat of the tree of life in their fallen condition and remain separated from Him for all of eternity.

Yet, God had a plan in place, even before Satan's sinister scheme of deception against Adam and Eve, and before He placed the sword at the entrance to the garden. He had a plan to solve the ultimate problem of sin ... the problem that had caused separation between God and man. God declared to the serpent in the garden, Satan, that He would solve this problem in time:

And I will put enmity between you and the woman, and between your offspring and hers; he will crush your head, and you will strike his heel." **Genesis 3:15 NIV**

Any crisis we face, whether it is a plague or any other disaster, is sent from the enemy to divide us, to separate us from each other and from God. But God will not be outsmarted by the enemy or be shut down by any sickness or crisis. His plan is superior, and everything else is inferior. Instead, God uses our crisis to remind us of the greatest story that has ever been told... the story of how a Savior defeated the sin that separated us from our Heavenly Father.

Our Sin was Cancelled on the Cross

During the height of social quarantine during the pandemic, it seemed like everything was cancelled: haircuts, handshakes, workouts, sporting events, concerts, Broadway, schools, daycare, and in-person church services.

But even in this, we can see the hand of Christ in every cancellation. God uses what the devil meant for evil to remind us of what He did to put an end to our separation from God.

> *He destroyed the record of the debt we owed, with its requirements that worked against us. He canceled it by nailing it to the cross.* ***Colossians 2:14 CEV***

Yes, two thousand years ago on a hill called Calvary, on a cross placed on top of Golgotha, my sin and your sin... was cancelled. Every bit of it. As far as the East is from the West, so far has He removed our transgressions from us!

Cancelled.

God had a plan to put end to the separation that made His heart sick, and so He sent His Son, our Savior Jesus Christ, to cancel our sin.

Not some of it, but all of it... paid in full!

But, somebody would say, that's not fair, that's not justice. You can't just let somebody off without punishment when they do something that is clearly wrong. And make no mistake about it, sin is wrong! It's not cute, it's not "culturally defined," it's not "politically incorrect"... and it's not fair for sin to go unpunished.

But sin did not go unpunished.

The good news is that justice was served and God's wrath was satisfied.

Surely He has borne our griefs And carried our sorrows; Yet we esteemed Him stricken, Smitten by God, and afflicted. But he was wounded for our transgressions, He was bruised for our iniquities; The chastisement for our peace was upon Him, And by His stripes we are healed. All we like sheep have gone astray; We have turned, every one, to his own way; And the Lord has laid on Him the iniquity of us all. He was oppressed and He was afflicted, Yet He opened not His mouth; He was led as a lamb to the slaughter, And as a sheep before its shearers is silent, So He opened not His mouth. He was taken from prison and from judgment, And who will declare His generation? For He was cut off from the land of the living; For the transgressions of My people He was stricken.

Yet it pleased the Lord to bruise Him; He has put Him to grief. When You make His soul an offering for sin, He shall see His seed, He shall prolong His days, And the pleasure of the Lord shall prosper in His hand. He shall see the labor of His soul, and be satisfied. **Isaiah 53:4-8, 10-11 NKJV**

Sin was punished in the worst way possible. The Holy Son of God, Jesus Christ, took our place and became a substitute for us; and the entire wrath of God was poured out on Him as punishment for the sin of mankind... past, present and future. It was a wrath so great so it caused Jesus to cry out, *"My God, my God, why hast Thou forsaken Me?"* But here is the good news... sin was not just punished, but God's judgment was satisfied in full.

The word "satisfied" in the original language is the strongest of all words used, and it would be better translated "satiated" (as in when you eat so much, you can't stand the thought of another bite cause it would make you throw up!) The punishment for sin placed upon Jesus was so great that it satiated God's wrath.

God is not punishing the world with the corona virus or any other crisis, for that matter. These things are from the devil... straight from the pit of Hell. The reason we know this is because God's wrath toward man's sin was satisfied in the work of Jesus Christ on the cross. The punishment Jesus bore was more than enough to deal with the sin that separated us from the Father and made His heart sick.

Our Curse Was Quarantined

The true contagion plaguing man is rarely thought about, or even talked about. It is the "Curse of the Law."

With sin came separation from God and a curse. The curse was poverty, sickness and spiritual death... all highly infectious, contagious and deadly.

And God said... *before I can put an end to separation, I've got to quarantine the curse.* He put the curse on one person (Jesus) and then quarantined that person in a tomb for three days and nights!

> *Christ has redeemed us from the curse of the law, having become a curse for us (for it is written, "Cursed is everyone who hangs on a tree"),...*
> **Galatians 3:13 NKJV**

The Curse of the Law was quarantined on the cross when Jesus became sin for us! On the cross, Jesus became the curse! He became poverty, sickness and was separated from the Father. God turned His back on Jesus, so that He could ultimately bring mankind back into relationship with Him.

For three days and nights He was quarantined in death, because on the cross, He became the curse.

But then, you know...

- The stone was rolled away
- He walked out of the tomb
- The tomb didn't stay empty

And He left some things in the tomb!

- He left our fear in the tomb
- He left our anxiety in the tomb
- He left our worry in the tomb
- He left our depression in the tomb
- He left our poverty in the tomb
- He left our sickness in the tomb

And He left our spiritual separation from God in the tomb!

Our "Spiritual" Distancing Was Destroyed

And Jesus cried out again with a loud voice, and yielded up His spirit. Then, behold, the veil of the temple was torn in two from top to bottom; and the earth quaked, and the rocks were split... **Matthew 27:50 NKJV**

Under the Old Covenant, the covenant in which sin was not cancelled, nor judgment satisfied, and the curse was not quarantined, God limited His manifest presence to a place in the Temple called the Holy of Holies.

The Holy of Holies was the location of precious objects of worship, including the Ark of the Covenant, and consequently, the Mercy Seat. Once a year on Yom Kippor (The Day of Atonement), the High Priest, and only the High Priest, could enter into the Holy of Holies without being struck dead. After careful cleansing and preparation, he would enter in and sprinkle blood on the Mercy Seat, as an offering for the atonement of sins of the people.

But atonement under the Old Testament was not forgiveness. Offering an animal blood sacrifice on Yom Kippor was is like paying the minimum payment on a credit card. The minimum payment keeps the credit card company from coming after you to collect on the debt, but it does little to cancel the debt.

So the High Priest would go once a year into the Holy of Holies to make this temporary blood sacrifice for sins. But in order to get into the Holy of Holies, he had to go behind an enormous woven veil; the Bible says it was between 45-60 feet high, and 4 inches thick! It guarded the presence of God.

Or rather, it protected sinful people from encountering the presence of a holy God.

And even though the High Priest was permitted to go into the Holy of Holies behind the veil on Yom Kippor, Jewish tradition tells us they always tied a rope around his waist, just in case he committed some error, fell dead, and had to have others drag him out. Everything had to be done perfectly. There was no gray area... the veil represented separation from God due to the sin of the people which was not cancelled, due to the judgment of God that was not satisfied... and the curse of the law which was not quarantined.

But look at what the Scripture says happened on the cross. It says:

Not with the blood of goats and calves, but with His own blood He entered the Most Holy Place once for all, having obtained eternal redemption. **Hebrews 9:12 NKJV**

What's that mean? It means Jesus, through His death on the cross, was both the High Priest AND the sacrifice!

And this sacrifice was different.

It wasn't the minimum payment on the credit card, it was the entire balance. It wiped out the debt. It was a once and for all sacrifice.

When His blood entered into the Holy of Holies in the heavenly tabernacle and was spilt on the Mercy Seat of God Almighty... the eternal significance of that offering showed up in the sacred place down in the earthly tabernacle.

The veil in the temple, that 45-60 foot, 4 inch thick veil of separation between our holy God and sinful man, was ripped... not from bottom to top, but from the top down to the bottom.

Not ripped by man, but by God Himself. It was the Almighty God of the universe reaching down with His massive, loving hands and tearing the veil in two, saying... *"I am sick of this separation! It is now time for Me to provide anyone who will with an all-access pass into My throne room, anytime they want to come!*

Let us therefore come boldly to the throne of grace, that we may obtain mercy and find grace to help in time of need. **Hebrews 4:16 NKJV**

Translation: You no longer need to come to God with fear and trepidation. Leave the rope outside. Don't worry that you aren't holy enough or deserving. Come boldly, even when you need mercy, and you will find grace to help in time of need. No more ropes. No more veils. No more separation. With that act of atonement our life with God was reopened!

What we have learned from COVID-19 in this lesson is that the concept of "social distancing" goes against the way we humans are created. We are made in God's image and are meant to be together in community. We learned that God went to great lengths to end the "spiritual separation" between Him and us, and He brought an end to the ultimate plague of sin and death. He ended our "curse" by the shed blood of Jesus Christ. Now, no matter what crisis we may face, or what regulations may keep us from contact with other people, we can come boldly to the Throne of Grace in our time of need. Selah!

LESSON SEVEN
Shut It Down

*Now it happened as they went that He entered a certain village; and a certain woman named Martha welcomed Him into her house. And she had a sister called Mary, who also sat at Jesus' feet and heard His word. But Martha was distracted with much serving, and she approached Him and said, "Lord, do You not care that my sister has left me to serve alone? Therefore tell her to help me." And Jesus answered and said to her, "Martha, Martha, you are worried and troubled about many things. But one thing is needed, and Mary has chosen that good part, which will not be taken away from her." **Luke 10:38-42 NKJV***

In this account, Martha is frantically running around the house trying to get things in place for the unexpected and unannounced luncheon with Jesus and His twelve disciples.

She's vacuuming, sweeping, making up the beds, picking up the toys, getting the dishes out of the sink, pulling together some leftovers, milking the goat, plucking the chicken, putting on the tea kettle, powdering her nose, corralling the kids, setting the table, running from one room to the next...

She's going hard. She's distracted with much serving. And her sister Mary is just chillin' at the feet of Jesus. These two sisters are living life at two completely different paces.

Martha's character is like our modern day, "pre-COVID pace" ... the New York Minute pace, the city that never sleeps pace, the taking the subway and then walking a few blocks as fast as you can with your cell phone in hand, head down, oblivious to the world around you, pace.

Mary's character is like the modern day "shelter in place pace."

Before our experience with COVID-19, we looked at Mary as the hero and Martha as the zero. We aspired to slow down and become like Mary... if we only had the time.

At first, it was such a blessing! But after being forced to "shelter in place" for weeks on end, most of us grew tired of acting like Mary, and wanted to get back to the fast pace of life. We wanted to get back to running the kids here and there, to having a daily commute, appointments, activities and juggling a million different things.

Back to life ... and back to reality.

But I would argue that Mary is still the hero in our story. What if in reality, God has collective said to all of us during this time of global pandemic... *Martha, Martha, you were way too distracted with 'non-essential' stuff!*

Although COVID-19 was never the plan nor the hand of God, He has and will continue to use it as a lesson, as a "Spiritual Forced Shut Down." The Martha in all of us must permanently slow down and the Mary in all of us must rebound.

Martha represents the fast pace of modern day distractions that ultimately lead many people away from God. Mary represents the pace of life that leads to experiencing God's miracles. So many of us miss out on the glory and power of God because we refuse to rest and enjoy what matters most.

To be sure, Martha has some wonderful attributes:

- She welcomed Jesus into her home
- She loved to serve others with excellence
- She cared about being neat and tidy, efficient and orderly

Our Martha life had some great qualities, too, but the fact is, you and I were never designed to do life at the frenetic pace that most of us have done it in the past. For many people, the "Martha pace" was such a part of life that we actually turned being overly busy into a kind of badge of honor.

Think about most of our conversations...

— How you doing? Busy.
— What's going on? Oh, just keeping busy.
— Sorry I'm late! I was just *so* busy.

We speak of "busy" as if it's the ultimate modern value. But what Jesus is telling Martha in the story, and what He is telling us today is that busy is not always better! In fact, busy can lead to a brokenness in our lives that manifests itself in so many unhealthy ways: anxiety, stress (which is the root cause of so many fatal illnesses); broken marriages; single parent families; latch-key kids; missed moments that we can never get back, and a barrenness of soul because we are just too busy for God!

It appears God is taking what the enemy meant for evil from the pandemic, and through a forced shut down, He is turning it around for our good so that we might rest, reflect and establish a healthier "new normal." Less like Martha... more like Mary.

God's Take on R.E.S.T.

Since the beginning of creation, God has put a premium on rest stops.

...so on the seventh day He rested from all His work. And God blessed the seventh day and made it holy, because on it He rested from all the work of creating that He had done. **Genesis 2:2 NIV**

God didn't rest because He was tired (the Scripture tells us God never gets tired or weary). Rather, He rested to give all of us "busy" people a pattern, or a rhythm of life that we need to follow so we don't get tipped over.

In fact, it's a commandment. God is so serious about this solution to our Martha pace of life, that He commands a regular, weekly "shut down" in Scripture:

> *Remember the Sabbath day by keeping it holy. Six days you shall labor and do all your work, but the seventh day is a Sabbath to the LORD your God. On it you shall not do any work, neither you, nor your son or daughter, nor your manservant or maidservant, nor your animals, nor the alien within your gates. For in six days the LORD made the heavens and the earth, the sea, and all that is in them, but he rested on the seventh day. Therefore the LORD blessed the Sabbath day and made it holy.* **Exodus 20:8 NKJV**

Resting on the Sabbath Day is one of the Ten Great Commandments. That means God put the importance of rest right up there with do not steal, do not murder, and do not commit adultery!

Some Bible scholars even think that when God gave the Ten Commandments to Moses, He was prioritizing them in order (greatest importance first). If that is true, it would mean that "resting," in God's eyes, was a higher priority than not stealing, murdering or committing adultery. Sounds strange, but if you think about it, when we are well-rested, we are usually able to think clearly enough not to steal, murder or commit adultery! So it makes sense...

But consider this: If you or I were God, "rest" would not even have made the list, because to us, "busy" is better.

In fact, we break this commandment more than any other, and without a feeling of guilt... don't we? If we were to steal, murder or commit adultery there is a heavy sense of guilt.

But if we work seven days a week, there is no guilt; rather just the opposite! There is a sense of accomplishment and even a sense of pride that says, *I'm so important that I don't even get a day off!*

However, God knew how man would react. In Exodus, He deals simply with these other commands and says, "You shall not...." But when it comes to keeping the Sabbath, resting one day a week... a weekly, forced shut down, God devotes an entire paragraph and closes loopholes! God is so serious about observing a day of rest, that before giving this commandment to the children of Israel, He peppers their hearts and minds concerning the importance of the Sabbath by giving them a visual example.

Just a few chapters prior to the Ten Commandments being handed down to the children of Israel, we find them wandering in the desert, complaining and grumbling that they have no food. And God says, *Okay, I'll feed you manna from heaven!*

> *... and in the morning there was a layer of dew around the camp. When the dew was gone, thin flakes like frost on the ground appeared on the desert floor.* **Exodus 16:13-14 NKJV**

God sent them "thin flakes like frost..." It was the original "Frosted Flakes" for breakfast! (*I think they're grrr...eat, but Israel did not!*) In fact, they looked at the flakes and said, *What is it?*

That's literally what the name "manna" means: "What is it?" So the next time you don't like what your spouse makes for dinner but you don't want to hurt their feelings, just look at it and say, "This is manna from heaven!"

Now here is the point...

Concerning the manna, God told the children of Israel to go out every morning and collect and eat ONLY as much as they needed for the day. That is, don't hoard. Don't stock your tent pantries to overflowing. Only get as much manna as you need for the day, because any more than that will spoil and rot.

But then He also told them that on the day just before the Sabbath day, they should collect two days' worth of manna. On this day, God promised that He would supernaturally prevent the manna from rotting, so that they would not have to go out to work.

Here's what the message of the Sabbath means for us today. God says if you trust Me by resting from all your labor one day a week, I will supernaturally touch your life and allow you to accomplish seven days of work in only six.

What?! God says, *I will do a supernatural work in your life if you shut it down one day a week!*

Amazing... God knew that the Israelites would become a great nation one day. He knew that they would build armies, open businesses, make money and become exporters of goods. They would be blessed and prospered, and become really successful, and with that, there would be temptation. Like us, they would be tempted to become infatuated with themselves, thinking that by working hard, they were the cause of their own success.

And so God challenged them, just like He still challenges us, to trust Him as their source by shutting it down one day a week to rest!

Isn't it interesting how God has given us two great resources in life... our time, and our money. With both of these resources, He has built-in reminders that He is our source. Regarding money, God says once a week bring your tithes and offerings into the local church, and remember that I am the source of every financial blessing. Regarding our time, God says, once a week shut it down, and remember that I am the source of your ability to be productive and prosperous.

In both cases, when you act according to His will... when you tithe and when you rest, He promises to do supernatural things in your life!

God sent us a clear message through the forced global shut down during 2020... we must be intentional about letting the "Mary" in us win out over the "Martha" in us, often enough, to live a healthy and balanced life. Don't view the act of resting as a handicap to keep you broke, but look at it as an opportunity to move from a Martha pace to a Mary pace.

Four Principles of R.E.S.T.

R... Reset Priorities

Looking again at the verse in Luke 10, everything Martha was doing could be considered "important." Opening up her home to Jesus... important; cleaning her house... important; cooking for her family... important; serving others... important.

Everything was ...important.

But Jesus said none of it was more important than sitting at His feet and learning from the Master. Even though Martha was doing important stuff, Mary was able to recognize and do more important things. Remember what Jesus said: *But one thing is needed, and Mary has chosen that good part.*

Choosing to invest in the most important things in life is all about resetting our priorities. God would much rather you have fewer material goods, than work too much, just to buy more stuff. God would rather you get passed up for a promotion, than miss watching your kids grow up. God would rather you be less affluent, than constantly anxious, less stressed, than more successful.

But rest is not about doing nothing and being lazy. It's not about sitting around in your house all day in your PJs being a couch potato; rather, it's about resetting priorities.

Mary said "no" to the good, so she could say "yes" to the great.

When Lisa and I first got married, she was the bread winner. She made three times what I made, because I had given up my career to go into the ministry. And then she got pregnant and we had to make some pretty serious decisions. She wanted to stay home and raise our children full-time. It was a priority for us, so that's the decision we made.

Here is what it meant for us... it meant going down to one car; it meant watching every dollar we spent; it meant not being able to go on vacation or eat out, and all that we loved to do.

But for us, it also meant having a happy home.

For us it meant she chose to do what she loved most – being there for her children, and not having to balance that with full-time, outside employment.

I realize that not everyone can choose to do that. But I also realize that some people would rather have all of the luxuries of life and refuse to even try.

Holy Shift!

Rest is about resetting our priorities, so that what's truly important is at the top of the list. God challenges our priorities during times of crisis like the forced economic shutdown of 2020. We begin to reset the priority of things like faith in God and family above empty pursuits of life; those things that lead to so many self-imposed struggles. Maybe even, there is a silver lining in crises like the pandemic. Maybe, just maybe, there will be a permanent "Holy Shift" in our priorities, back to what we've strayed from as a nation, and as a Church.

And when put our priorities in order, God's blessing always shows up!

> *But seek first the kingdom of God and His righteousness, and all these things shall be added to you.* ***Matthew 6:33 NKJV***

Most of us have heard of the highly successful fast food restaurant, Chick-fil-A, but we don't necessarily know the name of Truet Cathy, who is its founder and CEO.

Mr. Cathy is a devoted follower of Jesus Christ, and he made a decision when he founded Chick-fil-A, that his stores would not be open on Sunday. Sunday is the day he celebrates the Sabbath day, and he wanted to encourage his employees and customers to go to church and spend time with their family.

The experts advised him that his decision would be financial suicide, because Sunday is one of the busiest days of the week for the fast food industry. They declared that his stores would not survive. Nevertheless, Mr. Cathy trusted God, prioritized church and family, and shut down his restaurants every Sunday.

Did it cost him financially? Perhaps.

But what did he gain?

- He has a healthy marriage
- He is considered a wonderful father
- He is a youth worker in his church and loves it
- He is a man in good health (which is a supernatural act when you own a fast food chain!)

Oh, and by the way, he is a multi-millionaire, even though he is the only major fast food chain in America which shuts it down one day a week.

God did what God said He would do. He acted supernaturally in Truet's life, because Truet Cathy trusted Him, and one day a week, rested from all his labors. God's blessing showed up in his life because he chose to "R"... reset his priorities.

E... Enjoy Life!

When you think about our story of Mary and Martha, who do you envision enjoying life more? Who do you envision with a smile on her face? I see Mary, laughing, with a grin ear to ear, while Martha wears a scowl and a look that could kill as she angrily stares at Mary with Jesus.

Matter of fact, it is safe to say she was angry with both of them, when she said:

"Lord, do You not care that my sister has left me to serve alone? Therefore tell her to help me." **Luke 10:40 NKJV**

Jesus, why aren't you scolding her and telling her to get off of her blessed assurance and help me!! Martha was not exactly enjoying life. Here is what rest does... it helps you to enjoy the life you've been given. Did you realize that God wants you to enjoy life?

Pay attention to how the Amplified Version translates one of the most famous Scriptures in all of the Bible:

The thief comes only in order to steal and kill and destroy. I came that they may have and enjoy life, and have it in abundance [to the full, till it overflows]. **John 10:10 AMP**

God wants us to enjoy this life, and that's what resting from the Martha-paced lifestyle enables us to do. Remember Mary was the one with a smile on her face, and Martha was like a rude waitress; she was serving, but there was no smile and no joy, because she didn't know how to rest. Rest allows us to relax, laugh, and enjoy life.

A cheerful heart is good medicine, but a broken spirit saps a person's strength. **Proverbs 17:22 NLT**

Scientists have discovered that laughter relaxes the whole body, leaving muscles relaxed for up to 45 minutes after. It boosts the immune system, decreases stress hormones and increases immune cells and infection-fighting antibodies... so improves the body's resistance to disease.

Laughter triggers the release of endorphins. Endorphins promote an overall sense of well-being and can even temporarily relieve pain. It protects the heart and improves the function of blood vessels, increasing blood flow, which can then help protect you against a heart attack and other cardiovascular problems.

Laughter lightens anger's heavy load. Looking at the funny side of life can put problems into perspective and enable you to move on from confrontations without holding onto bitterness or resentment.

Laughter may even help you to live longer. A study in Norway found that people with a strong sense of humor outlived those who don't laugh as much. The difference was particularly notable for those battling cancer.

And let's not forget... Laughter burns calories.

Okay, it's no replacement for going to the gym... but still, it burns calories!

Rest means enjoying life.

Martha was overly engaged in the wrong things and so she was agitated and angry. Mary was restfully engaged in the best things and she was able to enjoy life.

S... Soul Care

In our story, Martha was working in the kitchen and Mary was sitting and listening at the feet of Jesus... a place she was familiar with. But prior to meeting Jesus, Mary had a pretty dark past. She was a young lady whose soul was stained, sick and separated... separated from her family and from God.

Stained by sin.

Mary was sick of being used, abused, undervalued and overlooked because she was the town prostitute.

But somewhere along the line she met Jesus, and He set her soul free, and gave back her dignity. He released her from her past, her guilt, her shame, and gave her a new identity as a child of God. He restored her to relationship with her family, cleansed her soul, and freed her from bondage to sin and death.

On another evening, Jesus was having dinner at the home of Simon the Pharisee. However, it appears that they only invited Jesus to trick him into saying something that they could use against Him.

When He arrived, they didn't greet Him with a holy kiss, they didn't anoint His head with oil, and they didn't wash His feet... which was the polite custom for receiving an honored guest.

Mary was watching the whole scene. When she couldn't stand how they dishonored Him any longer, she crashed the party and began to kiss His feet, wash them with her tears and dry them with her hair. She then broke open her alabaster box filled with costly perfume and anointed Him with it.

These powerful, religious men were aghast that Jesus could let this kind of sinful woman touch Him. They reasoned that if He really was a prophet, He would know this about her, and not allow her to interact with Him like this. But Mary had made a bee-line for the feet of Jesus in the presence of all these religious pretenders... simply because Jesus had restored her soul.

And now, back to our story above... Martha is working in the kitchen to prepare a meal to eat, and Mary is feeding her soul at the feet of Jesus. Martha is moving around at a frantic pace, focusing on everything but what truly was important. Martha didn't know the value of Jesus' presence, but Mary would never forget, because it was at His feet that her soul was restored.

Life takes a lot out of all of us... the hustle and bustle... the pain and heartache... the tears and the struggles. And even though many times we keep it moving, every battle takes a little piece. Sure, it makes us stronger, but it also takes from our strength. Over time, it mounts, and our souls must be replenished.

You can try to fix what's been broken on the inside by covering it up with worldly pursuits, or with any one of our culturally acceptable solutions. But there is only one cure that will bring about true healing, and that is time at the feet of Jesus. Time in His presence where there, and only there, you will find fullness of joy.

It's like the Psalmist wrote in Psalm 23:

The Lord is my shepherd; I shall not want. He makes me to lie down in green pastures; He leads me beside the still waters. He restores my soul;...
Psalm 23:1-3 NKJV

The context of this verse is a person walking through the valley of the shadow of death... that's life; that's the battles we go through while we live in this broken world. And as the Psalm says, money doesn't restore my soul. Work doesn't restore my soul. Success doesn't restore my soul. Expensive vacations don't restore my soul. Even accomplishments and accolades don't restore my soul.

He, and only He, restores my soul!

Mary knew this because of what she had been through in her life. She knew what Martha was too busy to discover... that it is only the Savior Who can restore our souls that get stripped by the struggles of this life.

T... Treasure the Moment

Jesus is in the house.

He and His disciples have stopped in to Martha and Mary's house for lunch. It's not every day that Jesus is over for lunch. Mary recognizes this is a special moment, but Martha is so busy, she is about to miss it.

Mary is saying this is a moment we can't get back... a moment we must treasure.

Mary is saying we are not going to lose the moment by having to do that or this or the other thing. We are going to put everything on hold so we can treasure the moment of focus on Jesus.

So what COVID-19 taught us in this lesson is that no crisis lasts forever. Soon enough it will be over. If we are not careful, we can lose our focus on Jesus, and our restful Mary pace and go back to the hustle, bustle and distractions of a Martha pace. Rest is important to God and we need to shut it down once a week whether in crisis or not. Treasure these moments of rest and singular focus on Jesus. It will be health and restoration for your body, soul and spirit, and is just what the Doctor ordered!

LESSON EIGHT
Faith Grows in Crisis

And as Moses lifted up the serpent in the wilderness, even so must the Son of Man be lifted up, that whoever believes in Him should not perish but have eternal life. For God so loved the world that He gave His only begotten Son, that whoever believes in Him should not perish but have everlasting life. **John 3:14-16 NKJV**

After leaving Egypt, the children of Israel were wandering about in the wilderness, and they experienced an outbreak of disease. It was a contagion in the form of deadly fiery serpents in the camp, whose sting was 100% fatal. As many of the children of Israel that were bitten, died.

Their situation was dire. They were lost, physically and spiritually. They complained against God and Moses... and where WAS God in their crisis, anyway?

But Moses prayed to the LORD and repented on behalf of the people, asking God for a cure.

Then the LORD said to Moses, "Make a fiery serpent, and set it on a pole; and it shall be that everyone who is bitten, when he looks at it, shall live." So Moses made a bronze serpent, and put it on a pole; and so it was, if a serpent had bitten anyone, when he looked at the bronze serpent, he lived. **Numbers 21:8-9 NKJV**

It's counterintuitive. The last thing you would think would heal these bitten, afflicted people would be a bronze sculpture of the very thing that was causing the crisis. And yet, from that very curse, God created a cure!

You may already know this, but medical science assures us that every "cure" has part of the "curse" in it. That is, every antidote for snake bite has some of the venom in it. Every vaccine for tropical disease has some of the bacteria in it. And any vaccine created for COVID-19 will have some of the coronavirus in it. As weird as it sounds, the cure always comes from the curse or, we can say, from the curse the cure emerges.

Vaccines work by exposing the immune system to small amounts of a virus or bacteria, so it can learn how to protect your body against that germ. Vaccines are made by scientists growing or generating parts of a germ, which are often weakened or inactivated to safely and effectively expose your body to that virus or bacteria. The cure comes from the curse.

There are so many ways this truth translates in Scripture: from the life of Joseph, we learn what the enemy meant for evil, God used for good. God used Joseph's brothers, Potiphar's wife, and the baker's betrayal to get Joseph from his home in Israel to the Egyptian palace... at just the right time to take control in a time of crisis. And God used Pharaoh and the land of Egypt to provide a safe place for the children of Israel to multiply greatly in number in order to become a mighty nation... large enough to take possession of the Promised Land that God had given them.

From the life of Paul: God took the Church's greatest persecutor and turned him into the Apostle Paul (the Church's greatest asset).

From the line of Jacob, a deceiver, and Rahab, a foreign prostitute, God brought forth His Son Jesus Christ. And from sin itself, God brought forth salvation.

But how does understanding this concept help us in our crisis?

The ultimate "curse" in our country is that in the past few decades, we have become broken, and are no longer one nation, united under God. Indeed, we have chosen sides against one another. We have embraced a kind of "tribalism" and we wear it as a badge of superiority against our opposite tribe.

We say things like:

- I am Republican... I am Democrat
- I am conservative... I am progressive
- I am white.. I am black... I am Latino... I am Asian
- I am religious... I am atheist... I am "spiritual"
- I am for this... I am against that

    .... and I am right!

Our leaders have also chosen their sides, and often cannot compromise. They fight, block, delay; they criticize and complain; they resort to name calling and hateful tweets. They push their political party's agenda at the expense of doing what's right and good for the people of this country as a whole.

Somewhere along the way we lost our core values: respect and honor for our elders and the wisdom they have gained; love and compassion for our neighbors who are struggling under burdens we don't have; the ability to honestly discuss and consider an opinion different than what we hold dear.

We've saturated our minds with high-tech screen-time that condenses our relationships into posts and texts and tweets and snaps, and have reduced our attention spans to video clips and sound bites.

As a nation, our moral compass has been spinning in all directions, as people in leadership are suddenly calling what's always been good, "evil", and what's always been evil, is now "good."

Like the Israelites in the wilderness... we have lost our way spiritually, and, with this latest

COVID crisis, we have been bitten by the Serpent that brings a curse.

No, this COVID virus is not from God. John 10:10 tells us of the serpent that brings this curse. His desire is to kill and destroy everything we hold dear. He wants to kill people, destroy the economy, pervert the educational system, silence the churches, and break up relationships. His goal is to eliminate freedom, cripple peace of mind, steal hope and joy, and extinguish love for our neighbors. But even so, what the enemy meant for evil, God has been turning for good. There are a few "cures" for our nation which have already started coming out the COVID crisis. They are not fully developed, but there are promising changes happening already.

The "Love Your Neighbor" Cure

Jesus said to him, 'YOU SHALL LOVE THE LORD YOUR GOD WITH ALL YOUR HEART, WITH ALL YOUR SOUL, AND WITH ALL YOUR MIND.' This is the first and great commandment. And the second is like it: 'YOU SHALL LOVE YOUR NEIGHBOR AS YOURSELF.' **Matthew 22:37-39 NKJV**

"Love your neighbor as yourself." This is the Mt. Everest of the Christian life, not "a" way, but THE way to treat others. Love them... treat them not as they *actually* treat you, but as you *would want* them to treat you... with goodness, kindness, understanding, charity, support, encouragement, prayer and hope. And during the COVID-19 crisis, as it often does, love rose to the surface first.

- Generosity in charitable donations went soaring
- Restaurants began supplying free food to first responders and front line workers
- Community outreaches blossomed to help those suddenly unemployed
- Neighbors began taking care of elderly neighbors

During the COVID-19 crisis, we instinctively returned to the "love your neighbor" cure. But we need to recognize it, and actively work to make sure we don't lose what we have gained.

The "We Are Better Together" Cure

Two are better than one, Because they have a good reward for their labor. ***Ecclesiastes 4:9 NKJV***

COVID-19 caused us to suddenly have a common enemy, albeit an unseen one. Generally speaking, having a common enemy causes us to release the power of everyone pulling in the same direction. To some degree, we have seen Democrats working together with Republicans in Congress for economic relief. We have seen private and public sector partnerships formed. We have seen state governments working together with the Federal government, churches working with community leaders... not fighting against one another, but working with one another. What power we have when we all pull together in one direction!

It's synergistic... the sum of the whole is greater than the parts.

Take the concept of horsepower in engines. One unit of power creates one "horsepower," but two units create not two, but three "horsepower," synergistically.

We are better together!

When we pull together there is nothing we cannot accomplish.

- When two pray together... God answers!
- When husband and wife parent in agreement, kids grow strong and sure
- When Church and community work toward common goals, cities prosper
- When generations, young and old, pull together and share vision and wisdom, the future is transformed

Working together, pulling together, living together, loving together... we are just better together. Let's never go back!

The "Responsibility of Leaders" Cure

*...For everyone to whom much is given, from him much will be required; and to whom much has been committed, of him they will ask the more. **Luke 12:48 NKJV***

It is the responsibility of a leader to protect the people under his or her care. Is there any greater example than Jesus who the Scripture said laid down his life for us! To protect us, serve us and save us!

This was the best thing we have seen come out of the COVID crisis... seeing leaders rise up, work together to help businesses, hourly workers, and anyone affected by the shutdown. During this time we have seen that true leadership is not about power, prestige, or politics... it's about people! So let's never go back!

The "Grateful For What We Have" Cure

In everything give thanks: for this is the will of God in Christ Jesus concerning you. **1 Thessalonians 5:18 NKJV**

During a crisis, it can be easy to focus on all the things that are going wrong. But one of the "cures" that we've seen from COVID-19 is that we have been given an opportunity to become aware of, and be thankful for, the things that matter the most: family and quality time at home, working from home with no stressful morning commute, and reconnecting with a spouse. Those who remained employed when others around didn't, have gained a whole new appreciation for their jobs. Some have been so grateful for a pension, a savings account, or generous family members. We've been thankful for the technology we have to hold church online and not miss a beat.

And we know that all things work together for good to those who love God, to those who are the called according to His purpose. **Romans 8:28 NKJV**

That means, we all must be intentional in looking, in any situation or crisis, for the good that God wants to do. When you tap into the "grateful for what you have" cure, it combats fear, anxiety, worry, depression and all the rest.

Gratitude is a "cure" that has come about from the curse of COVID-19. Let's not go back.

The "God Was at Work Before" Cure

*...for it is God who works in you both to will and to do for His good pleasure. **Philippians 2:13 NKJV...***

God is working now, but He was also working before, to enable us to get through. Nothing catches God by surprise! Prior to COVID-19, the United States had the best economy in its history; the unemployment was the lowest ever, the stock mark market was the highest ever... all economic indicators were strong, strong, strong.

Was it coincidence or God working? I believe it was God making us strong enough to withstand this storm and get to the other side.

In our church, we had to get our finances in order in 2019 for a mortgage refinance. That helped us to be ready... God was working!

We spent several years and concentrated our efforts to build our online church experience and social media platforms so that we did not miss a beat when the church was shut down... God was working!

Society itself has been changing in such a way that we could survive the COVID-19 crisis... including Amazon.com shopping, Instacart grocery deliveries, TeleMed doctor visits, Online Distance Learning, Zoom business meetings... God was working!

He works before, He works during and He will get us through any crisis! He always works on our behalf. God is for us, not against us... we will not be afraid. That is another "cure" we have from COVID-19... We recognize that God was at work before. Let's not go back.

The "Prayer Changes Things" Cure

...if My people who are called by My name will humble themselves, and pray and seek My face, and turn from their wicked ways, then I will hear from heaven, and will forgive their sin and heal their land. ***2 Chronicles 7:14 NKJV***

Prayer changes things. It moves the hand that moves the universe. Prayer invites Heaven and all its resources to intervene in a situation. It's the breeding ground for a turn around. Prayer causes the sun to stand still...

Prayer shuts the mouth of financial lions, and saves us from life's fiery furnaces. It opens the blind eyes of political leaders and unstops the deaf ears of unsaved loved ones. Prayer brings miraculous provision during impossible situations, and multiplies scarcity into riches like fishes and loaves.

Prayer can change the course of nations. One of the cures from COVID-19 has been a widespread return to prayer by the Church of the Living God. When the Church prays, God responds. Let's not go back.

The "Jesus is Lord" Cure

*"And as Moses lifted up the serpent in the wilderness, even so must the Son of Man be lifted up, that whoever believes in Him should not perish but have eternal life. For God so loved the world that He gave His only begotten Son, that whoever believes in Him should not perish but have everlasting life." **John 3:14-16 NKJV***

Notice the link between the serpent on the pole, and our Savior on the cross. Jesus, the sinless Son of God, became sin for us and took our place on that cross. He became the curse of death so that we could have the cure of eternal life. The Scripture puts it like this...

For He made Him who knew no sin to be sin for us, that we might become the righteousness of God in Him. **2 Corinthians 5:21 NKJV**

What COVID-19 has taught us in this lesson is that a crisis is an opportunity to grow our faith exponentially. When we place our faith in Christ, He can cause a "cure" to come out of any crisis, and we have seen many such "cures" begin developing in our nation through this experience. COVID-19 also exposed, more than ever before, the ultimate reality of sin. Though this crisis, we realized that Jesus, the Savior on the cross, is the real cure our world needs in every situation. Church, let's never go back!

LESSON NINE
Relationships Matter

When Jesus therefore saw His mother, and the disciple whom He loved standing by, He said to His mother, "Woman, behold your son!" Then He said to the disciple, "Behold your mother!" And from that hour that disciple took her to his own home. **John 19:26-27 NKJV**

During times of crisis, and especially those trying times that last longer than expected, it is common for many of us to struggle with the question... *does God really love me?*

- When I lose my job – does God really love me?
- When I get sick – does God really love me?
- When my loved one passes on – does God really love me?
- When I watch the world around me shut down and so many struggle – does God really love me?
- When my marriage is struggling – does God really love me?

- When I'm addicted and can't break free –
  does God really love me?

But then we come to the cross, Jesus answers
the age old question – Lord, how much do you
love me? *This much,* He says, as He stretches out
His arms and dies.

Jesus said very little during His death on the
Cross, so this interaction between Jesus, Mary
and the young disciple John is certainly
significant. Interestingly enough, though, it is
only recorded in the Gospel of John. And it is
perhaps least thought of among the final seven
sayings of Jesus from the cross.

But yet its message is profound in how it gives
us a poignant perspective of just how much He
loves you and me.

How John Loved Jesus

*When Jesus therefore saw His mother, and the disciple
whom He loved standing by...* **John 19:26 NKJV**

John describes himself as the "disciple whom Jesus loved." What a great way to see yourself! Not as the disciple who struggles, or the disciple who doubts. Not as the disciple who makes mistakes. After all, he was one who wanted to call down fire from heaven to destroy a town that had rejected Jesus! He was also one who wanted to be elevated and honored above the others in heaven by sitting at Jesus' right hand. He could have viewed himself solely through his mistakes and circumstances, but instead, he saw himself as the disciple whom Jesus loved.

John's faith was rooted and grounded in the truth that he was loved by Almighty God. And because he saw himself as loved, he was able to stand for Christ when all the other disciples scattered in fear.

No other disciple from the twelve was there at his feet when Jesus was crucified... only John. Peter attempted to stay, but when the struggle got real, he wasn't able to stand.

But not John. John stood when everyone else scattered.

Crisis will thin out a crowd. Crisis will show you what you are made of, and reveal your character: what and who you really love, and who really loves you.

The truth is, we really do get forged in the fire!

Strength to Stand

There is a standing power that comes from knowing that God loves us. It doesn't mean we always understand everything that happens in life, but it does mean we will hold up under pressure. It does mean there will be a grace to keep grinding when life beckons us to give up, and a supernatural strength to keep standing when life shouts "shrink back!"

...and having done all, to stand. ***Ephesians 6:13 NKJV***

- Stand, knowing that God loves you
- Stand, knowing that God is for you

- Stand, knowing that He has your best interest in mind
- Stand, knowing that His plan for you is better than your plan for yourself
- Stand, knowing that you may not see it now, but He will make a way

There is a standing power in knowing that He loves you and me! John the disciple loved Jesus and was able to stand, because He knew how much Jesus loved him.

How Mary Loved Jesus

A cursory look at the life of Mary, the mother of Jesus, could lead one to look with eyes of envy, as the angel called her "highly favored" and "blessed among women," to which I would say... look again!

You would think... what an amazing thing to be the mother of Jesus! She must have gotten so many compliments when He was growing up:

- Jesus was so well-behaved at school today
- Jesus got 100% on all His tests again this week
- Jesus won the Christian character award in class
- Jesus turned the other cheek even though He was in the right
- Jesus was such a peacemaker today
- I wish I had a child like Jesus, He never gives you any trouble Mary

... except when she had to endure the scandal, and being thought of as promiscuous for being pregnant before marriage. Except when she had to hear the whispered comments as He grew up... *I wonder if he is really Joseph's boy.* And except when, at the age of twelve, He stayed at the temple in Jerusalem talking to rabbis for three days, when His whole family had set off for home. Except when she had to deal with her neighbors saying He was demon possessed and a false teacher from the devil. Except when she watched religious leaders constantly trying to trick Him, accuse Him and kill Him.

And of course, except when she had to endure watching her baby boy being charged for a crime He didn't commit, being unjustly sentenced, and hung in shame on a cross.

What sacrifices she made.

What unwavering love she had.

What a picture of a mother's love.

When everyone around Him hated Him, talked about Him, plotted against Him, ostracized Him... she loved Him.

Mary endured crisis after crisis, because she loved Him.

How Jesus Loved Mary and John

Here He was, hanging on the cross being crucified, and yet He cared about what would happen to His mother.

He had nails in His hands and feet. His back had been completely shredded with a Roman whip. His face was swollen from being beaten by soldiers. His was wearing a crown made from thorns. He was struggling just to breathe.

And through bleeding lips, He says:

"Woman, behold your son!" Then He said to the disciple, "Behold your mother!" **John 19:26-27 NKJV**

Of all the things to think about while on the cross, He thinks about entrusting His mother's future to His friend.

Most Bible scholars agree that, by this time in Jesus' life, Joseph had passed on. In Jewish tradition, Jesus as the eldest son, had the responsibility of caring for his widowed mother. In fact, widows were dependent on their eldest sons to survive, and it was the high honor of any eldest son to take care of his mother for the rest of his life.

And here was Jesus on the cross, still ensuring that His mother will be taken care of.

Oh, how He loved His mother!

But interestingly enough, He doesn't entrust His mother's care to His brother James, or one of His other brothers. Yes, He had other siblings!

"Isn't this the carpenter's son? Isn't his mother's name Mary, and aren't his brothers James, Joseph, Simon and Judas? **Matthew 13:55 NIV**

Why didn't Jesus entrust His mother to one of His brothers, as would have been the custom? Simply put, at that time, none of His brothers were believers. In fact, it appears they didn't get saved until after the resurrection proved, beyond doubt, the true identity of Jesus as the Son of God. Imagine living in the house of Jesus, growing up with Jesus and not realizing who He is!

So, Jesus entrusts His mother's care to His most trusted friend, the only one whose heart was loyal enough to remain standing at the foot of the cross, when everyone else scattered in fear.

John stood with Him, and for that reason, Jesus entrusted His precious mother to his care. And John without hesitation, without regard for the cost or the inconvenience, from that moment the Scripture says took her into His home.

Oh how He loved John. And oh, how He loved Mary.

Many have called Jesus' third utterance from the cross, "the Word of Relationship," that is, the word that brought Mary and John into a new relationship with one another. And make no mistake about it, we were not meant to be socially distant or in isolation. We were created to be in relationship with one another, just as we are meant to be in relationship with Him. Jesus wants to give you hope in the midst of despair, eternal hope by bringing you into right relationship with Him, because of His great love for you.

Jesus to Calvary did go,
His love for sinners to show.
What He did there
brought hope from despair.
Oh, how He loves you;
Oh, how He loves me;
Oh, how He loves you and me!

~Kurt Kaiser

So the lesson we have learned here from COVID-19 is that relationships truly matter. God cares about how we treat one another. He cares if we take care of those in need. And He cares that we have a complete understanding of God's love for us. In fact, we love Him because He first loved us. And we can love others during troubled times, because He loves us at all times.

LESSON TEN
Make Lemonade

When David and his men reached Ziklag, they found it destroyed by fire and their wives and sons and daughters taken captive. So David and his men wept aloud until they had no strength left to weep. David's two wives had been captured—Ahinoam of Jezreel and Abigail, the widow of Nabal of Carmel. David was greatly distressed because the men were talking of stoning him; each one was bitter in spirit because of his sons and daughters. But David found strength in the Lord his God. ***1 Samuel 30:3-6 NIV***

Lemons by themselves are bitter. When you bite into a lemon, your entire face gets, well... nasty. There's no controlling it. But when you take the lemons and add sugar, water and ice ... everything changes. It becomes the perfect refreshing drink for a hot summer day... lemonade! With the right ingredients, you go from "bitter face" to "better face."

During crises like COVID-19 many people have been dealt bitter lemons: the loss of a job; a business that has gone up in smoke; or the death of a loved one. And when the time comes to pick up the pieces and move forward, often we are at a loss at where to start first. It is crucial to focus a bit on the process of restoration, because the truth is, life deals everyone lemons some of the time.

In the text, David and his men had been dealt a lemon of epic proportions. While they were away on a mission, their homes had been destroyed by an enemy, and their wives and children had been taken captive. In a moment of time, their lives and everything that truly mattered to them had gone up in smoke. David's men reacted as anyone normally would. They were so hurt and angry that they blamed their leader, David, and wanted to kill him in revenge. Everybody always wants someone to blame when life deals us lemons. Unfortunately, it's one of the ways we cope that, in the end, steals our hope.

Each one of these men was "bitter in spirit." That is, the "lemon" life dealt to them on the outside got buried deep within them on the inside. They were angry and hurt, thinking negatively, accusing, looking for fault, looking to place blame. They were overwhelmed, to the point where they had no strength left and each one of them became bitter in spirit.

But, in the face of the same "lemon," the same circumstances and the same pain, the Bible says David "found strength in the Lord." One popular translation of this passage is that David encouraged himself in the Lord.

This group of mighty men (tough, strong, and seemingly invincible), got dealt some pretty bad lemons, and they all stood at an intersection of decision: the intersection of "bitter road" and "better road."

It's an intersection of decision we all have to face at some point in our lives. What do you do when you stand at that intersection – do you bite the lemon, or do you make lemonade? Most importantly, how to you move forward afterward?

Realize You Have a Choice

When you find yourself at this intersection of decision, realize that although it may not seem like you have any option, you do indeed have a choice about which road you are going to go down. Always. You have a choice to be a lemon head or a lemonade drinker.

People, government, and authorities, can take certain freedoms away from us, but the one power we always have control over is our power to choose. Remember the words of Holocaust survivor Viktor Frankle, "The greatest of all human freedoms is to choose one's attitude in any given circumstances."

In other words, our greatest power is our power to choose. Scripture puts it like this:

This day I call the heavens and the earth as witnesses against you that I have set before you life and death, blessings and curses. Now choose life, so that you and your children may live. **Deuteronomy 30:19 NIV**

We can't choose whether or not we receive lemons in life, but we can choose how we respond to them and what road we will travel down: bitter road or better road.

Oftentimes, people who have gone down bitter road will justify themselves in their pain, and say... well, you just don't understand because you have never had anything bad like this happen to you. Or, it's easy for you to say, because you're not going through it like I am.

Enter David and his mighty men (all of whom experienced the same terrible circumstances: houses burned down, wives and kids captured). It really doesn't get much worse than that.

Each one of these men, except David, chose bitter road. David chose better road, because there is a supernatural strength that we can find in the Lord. He gives strength to the weary and increases the power of the weak. He is near to the brokenhearted. In times of trouble, He becomes our strength, in times of weakness, His grace fortifies us and carries us through. When we can't stand, He picks us up. When we can't fight, He fights for us. When depression covers us like a dark cloud... He is the glory and the lifter of our heads.

There is a strength that comes from the Lord. And it's available to you, if you choose it. Don't let the enemy convince you that you can't choose.

Or that you are stuck with a bitter portion. The reality is that you can choose, with the help of the Lord, and better days are ahead; a brighter future is in store. Weeping may endure for a season, but joy comes in the morning.

However, the normal response to crisis and tragedy, the natural human response to life dealing out lemons, is to get bitter. Our first reaction to bitter things is to bark and bite, and attack. It's the reason Jesus spent so much time teaching us to return good for evil, blessing for cursing, and to turn the other cheek.

But even though it's natural (trust me on this, been there, done that, got the T-shirt), it's the wrong choice. The further you go down bitter road, the more encumbered and weighty your spirit becomes, and the more grumpy and irritable and unhappy and mad at the world you get.

And the thing is, going down bitter road is a subtle choice. That is, nobody sets out and says, I think I'll go down bitter road today. I think I'll waste my life being hurt and angry and grumpy.

It's subtle. The bitter root begins under the surface, in a dark, secret place, a wound in your spirit that no one can see. At first nobody knows how you feel, and you're not going to complain because you know it doesn't change a thing. You want to act mature, resilient, not petty or childish. You don't want to discuss what's eating at you. You don't want to be vulnerable with others. You don't want to ask for help to cope with the pain... but under the surface of your carefully crafted façade, bitterness is quietly taking root.

See to it that no one falls short of the grace of God and that no bitter root grows up to cause trouble and defile many. **Hebrews 12:15 NIV**

"See to it..." Those are some pretty aggressive words that reinforce the truth that we can opt off of bitter road; or better yet, *choose* not to travel down it at all.

"See to it..." In other words we have the responsibility to war against the root of bitterness, because it is a spiritual cancer!

We must understand its power, because bitterness spreads like wildfire and causes lots of trouble for our lives and for those around us. The Word says it may start in private, but it doesn't stay private. It will eventually spring up from your spirit and everyone will be affected by it. That is, it starts showing up in your attitude and decisions, in your relationships... or on your job. And it contaminates everything: your outlook on life, your family and friendships, your health. Everything. It spreads like a virus. It corrupts what is good, and destroys your joy. It creates emotional baggage and faintly concealed rage... and in short, the Scripture puts it best when it says, "the bitter root grows up and causes trouble and defiles many."

The bitter road is always the wrong road to choose, even though sadly, it's the wide road that most people do indeed choose.

Go in through the narrow gate. The gate to destruction is wide, and the road that leads there is easy to follow. A lot of people go through that gate. But the gate to life is very narrow. The road that leads there is so hard to follow that only a few people find it. **Matthew 7:13-14 CEV**

There is a famous poem by Robert Frost called *The Road Not Taken* that illustrates this point beautifully.

Two roads diverged in a yellow wood,
And sorry I could not travel both
And be one traveler, long I stood
And looked down one as far as I could
To where it bent in the undergrowth;

Then took the other, as just as fair,
And having perhaps the better claim,
Because it was grassy and wanted wear;
Though as for that the passing there
Had worn them really about the same,

And both that morning equally lay
In leaves no step had trodden black.
Oh, I kept the first for another day!
Yet knowing how way leads on to way,
I doubted if I should ever come back.

I shall be telling this with a sigh
Somewhere ages and ages hence:
Two roads diverged in a wood, and I—
I took the one less traveled by,
And that has made all the difference.

Taking the right road makes all the difference. And make no mistake about it, the narrow road, the better road, is the right road!

On better road, people are much happier, more at ease, less likely to be offended, at peace, rational, unstuck, able to move forward... as difficult as it can be sometimes. Better road is just better.

There is restoration for your soul on better road. There's healing on better road. There's heart mending, comfort, and peace that passes all understanding on better road. There is "double for your trouble" on better road, and grace to keep grinding. There's help, meaning, and purpose on better road. There is even a repurposing of your pain on better road.

Remember, David chose better road, when his men choose bitter road. Was it easy? No – bitter road was easy. But David found his strength in the Lord, and here is what happened next...

David recovered everything the Amalekites had taken, including his two wives. **1 Samuel 30:18 NIV**

It's only when you choose to go down better road that God can take all the bad that has happened and turn it around for the good, according to Romans 8:28. It's only by choosing better road that you'll find recovery, restoration and future success. It's where God rights wrongs and takes the sting out the pain. It's where God works through the evil circumstances brought by the enemy, and the lemons that life throws our way, and puts in some sugar, water and ice and begins to refresh us.

You have to trust Him, and put it in His hands. Remember the story of the miraculous multiplication the loaves and fishes that started as a little boy's lunch and fed a crowd of 5000 families?

Jesus then took the loaves, gave thanks, and distributed to those who were seated as much as they wanted. He did the same with the fish. **John 6:11 NIV**

So how did the miracle happen? What they started with (five loaves and two little fish), wound up in the hands of Jesus. You see, when we choose to take life's lemons and put them in the hands of Jesus, those nail-scarred hands go to work... those same hands that took dirt and made the shell of the first man; those hands that cleansed leprous skin and restored sight to blind eyes, that reached out and picked up a woman cast to the ground for adultery.

It was those hands that took a little boy's lunch and turned it into an "all you can eat buffet" for thousands of His followers.

And He is waiting to get His hands on your mess, so He can turn that mess into something miraculous. You may not know how He does it, but when you put life's lemons in His hands, He adds the water, the ice and the sugar.

God blesses the better choice!

Why Me?

"Why me?" is a common and normal question to ask as we process through the lemons of life. And God understands that question. He doesn't get angry or mad, or upset with us for processing that way. In fact, many of God's generals questioned their lemons, including, at times, David himself.

How long, O Lord? Will You forget me forever? How long will You hide Your face from me? How long shall I take counsel in my soul, Having sorrow in my heart daily? How long will my enemy be exalted over me? **Psalm 13:1-2 NKJV**

David was having trouble processing the "why me" question.

Even Jesus on the cross asked it when He said, "My God, my God, why have You forsaken Me?" This means God understands the pain of life's lemons... personally. So "why me?" is not the wrong question because it will draw God's anger. No, if anything, it draws God's grace and mercy.

Instead, it's the wrong question because if we dwell on "why me?" too long, it leaves us stuck in the pain and paralyzed from moving forward. Focusing on why, in a world that isn't always fair, can and often does cause us to dull the pain the wrong way. So what is the right way?

Remember the account of Jesus on the cross. One of the seven things He said was, "I thirst."

After this, Jesus, knowing that all was now finished, said (to fulfill the Scripture), "I thirst." A jar full of sour wine stood there, so they put a sponge full of the sour wine on a hyssop branch and held it to His mouth. When Jesus had received the sour wine, He said, "It is finished," and He bowed His head and gave up His spirit. **John 19:28-30 ESV**

Imagine that... Jesus, the God who made the oceans, got thirsty... for you and me.

They offered Him some sour wine on a stick.

Sour wine was usually mixed with myrrh, and was used as an anesthetic for the person being crucified so they wouldn't feel as much pain. It was usually offered in compassion by the women who hung around the cross. But the Scripture states that Jesus refused to take it, because there is a wrong way to dull the pain. And clearly, Jesus wouldn't allow the pain to stand in the way of the rest of God's plan.

Certain ways of dulling the pain from life's lemons will stop you from finishing what God has planned for you to do. No matter where you are in life, He's still got more for you to do. Don't let "why me?" lead you down bitter road and cause you to try to dull the pain in an unproductive way.

Remember, "why me?" will lead you to anesthetize the pain by avoidance, procrastination or by pretending it doesn't it exist. "Why me?" will lead you to anesthetize the pain with drugs and alcohol, fornication or any other addictive trap... that doesn't actually dull the pain at all. It's the bait of Satan on a stick. Don't take the bait of "why me." There's a better way to deal with the pain... look instead to what God can do.

The right focus is, "Okay God, what now? What can You do with what I've been through?" The right focus is to look instead to what God can do. That is, to declare, "God I'm going to keep serving people as I always have and I love to do... and to trust You to take my pain and repurpose it. I trust You to take my pain and point me in the right direction, and turn it around so that I can help others."

"Lord, I trust You to take my pain and give me a platform for healing... and allow me to kick the snot out of the devil that sent it."

"God, I'm not focusing on "why me," but by Your grace, I'm focusing on what now and what You can do though this!"

Look instead to what God can do! That's how you make lemonade.

So today, I raise my glass to every one of you that has been dealt a lemon in life, in whatever crisis you have faced, and I prophetically declare over you, that God is going to give you a lemonade stand in the presence of your enemy, that is going to give you a supernatural strength! I declare it in Jesus' name!

If you receive it, say "Amen!"

All of these lessons we have learned from the experience of COVID-19 are available to you today to face any challenge, test, trial or crisis that may come in the future. However, there is one condition that must be met. You must be in Christ as a child of God to receive His benefits, protections and promises. And to do that you must repent (be sorry for, and turn away from) your sins, and receive Him into your heart.

Have you done that? Have you made Jesus Christ Lord and Savior of your life? If not, you can become a child of God today. Just pray this short prayer, and believe it:

Father God, I come to You in the Name of Jesus Christ, Your Son. I believe that He died for me and that He was resurrected from the dead. I believe He is alive right now and is Lord over all creation. I put my trust in Jesus Christ as my Savior and I repent of my sins. Lord, send your Holy Spirit into my heart, cleanse me of all sin, fill me with the righteousness of Christ. Help me to walk according to Your ways and follow You in every area of my life. Thank You, and I know I will never be the same! Amen.

If you just prayed that prayer for the first time, welcome to the family of God! He is now your Father and will help you every step of the way. Start by reading your Bible and attending a local, Bible-believing church. Pray and fellowship with God every day... and trust Him to make lemonade out of every one of life's lemons!

Other Books by Frank Santora

- *After You Die: Unveiling the Mysteries of Heaven*
- *Turn It Around: A Different Direction for a New Life*
- *Identity Crisis: Seeing Yourself as God Sees You*

The Mini-Library Collection

- *Speak Life to Your Dreams*
- *Swipe Left: How to Recognize Toxic People*
- *Your Giant is Going Down*
- *30 Minutes to Pizza: Praying to Get Results*
- *Investing in Your Destiny*
- *The Benefits of an Enemy*
- *Stay Woke: The Keto Diet for Your Mind*
- *The New York Minute Devotional*

Made in the USA
Middletown, DE
30 July 2020